sun signs
& soul mates

About the Author

Linda George (New Zealand) has been a professional astrologer for over twenty years, and has had a weekly astrology segment on morning television. Her first book, *Heart Rules*, about relationship consciousness and understanding relationships from a soul perspective, was a finalist in the mind/body/spirit genre of the Ashton Wylie awards for spiritual literature. The mother of four children, Linda has also worked as a journalist and in public relations.

To Write to the Author

If you wish to contact the author or would like more information about this book, please write to the author in care of Llewellyn Worldwide and we will forward your request. Both the author and publisher appreciate hearing from you and learning of your enjoyment of this book and how it has helped you. Llewellyn Worldwide cannot guarantee that every letter written to the author can be answered, but all will be forwarded. Please write to:

Linda George
℅ Llewellyn Worldwide
2143 Wooddale Drive, Dept. 978-0-7387-1558-2
Woodbury, MN 55125-2989, U.S.A.
Please enclose a self-addressed stamped envelope for reply,
or $1.00 to cover costs. If outside the U.S.A., enclose
an international postal reply coupon.

Many of Llewellyn's authors have websites with additional information and resources. For more information, please visit our website at http://www.llewellyn.com.

LINDA GEORGE

sun signs
& soul mates

An Astrological Guide to Relationships

Llewellyn Publications
Woodbury, Minnesota

First Edition
First Printing, 2009

Book design by Steffani Sawyer
Editing by Brett Fechheimer
Cover art © 2009 Digital Vision/PunchStock
Cover design by Ellen Dahl
Llewellyn is a registered trademark of Llewellyn Worldwide, Ltd.

Library of Congress Cataloging-in-Publication Data
George, Linda, 1961–
  Sun signs & soul mates : an astrological guide to relationships /Linda George.
— 1st ed.
    p. cm.
  Includes bibliographical references (p.   ).
  ISBN 978-0-7387-1558-2
  1. Astrology. 2. Interpersonal relations—Miscellanea. 3. Soul mates. I. Title.
II. Title: Sun signs and soul mates.
  BF1729.P8G46 2009
  133.5'864677—dc22
                    2009007261

Llewellyn Worldwide does not participate in, endorse, or have any authority or responsibility concerning private business transactions between our authors and the public.
  All mail addressed to the author is forwarded but the publisher cannot, unless specifically instructed by the author, give out an address or phone number.
  Any Internet references contained in this work are current at publication time, but the publisher cannot guarantee that a specific location will continue to be maintained. Please refer to the publisher's website for links to authors' websites and other sources.

Llewellyn Publications
A Division of Llewellyn Worldwide, Ltd.
2143 Wooddale Drive, Dept. 978-0-7387-1558-2
Woodbury, Minnesota 55125-2989, U.S.A.
www.llewellyn.com

Printed in the United States of America

Other books by Linda George

Heart Rules

To Roger, true mate of my Soul . . .
Thank you for making me whole

And my kids,
Elliot, Lee, Nina, and Reid,
No words can say how much I love you all
I treasure our journey together in this life . . .
Thank you for being the special Souls you are,
and for picking me!

Contents

Introduction:
We Are the Stars on Earth

After my death, the molecules of my being
will return to the earth and sky.
They came from the stars.
I am of the stars.
—Charles Lindbergh

The dance along the artery
The circulation of the lymph
Are figured in the drift of stars.
—T. S. Eliot

We are creatures of the cosmos. We came from the stars; our earth came from the stars. Before the "Big Bang"—the outbreath of God—we were part of the One. And so it is that we are still connected. We share the same fabric of the universe as the stars and the planets. There are large spaces between us, but we remain aspects of the Infinite. We resonate to the same music, the music of the cosmos, because we *are* the cosmos. We exist as individual sparks within the Mind of God—the Source of all that is, the field of consciousness, where we have the freedom to think, to create, and to participate consciously in our own evolution. The Mind of God is the intelligence of the cosmos, and we are part of that intelligence.

The universe, in its unimaginable immensity and diversity, is not only "out there"—it is "in here," in us, too. The vastness of space is perfectly replicated in the interior space of our own bodies. Our hearts are miniature suns—central coordinators of our physical and spiritual bodies. Our blood courses with molecules, the same ones that dance in distant stars. We are physical beings, and we are, at the same time, divine. In us, physical matter, the stuff of the visible universe, meets the faster vibrating energy of spirit, the invisible universe. Our embodiment on this planet is a temporary affair, but our souls are infinite and eternal. We are the form within the formless. We are the finite within the Infinite.

All the spiritual traditions the planet has known have their own versions of eternal life. Belief in the continuation of life beyond the physical is the one constant of the spiritual seeker. Scientific discoveries in quantum physics are bringing us closer to the spirituality of the ancient wisdom keepers, and the knowledge being revealed to us is that there is a part of us connected to the Infinite (the eternal), and we can access it through our consciousness. Consciousness, the eternal flame within each of us, is our bridge to our own higher selves and to the formless.

This book approaches consciousness in an holistic way. It offers a cosmic perspective that embraces the energy of the times we find ourselves living in. A time when we find Uranus, ruler of astrology, moving through Pisces; when boundaries are dissolving and people are learning about the nature of the field that connects all. This book is not as much about astrology as it is about the soul, which is an aspect of the divine, the God-force, the Supreme Intelligence, brought to an individualized focus in us. It is known, too, as the higher self. The soul, or higher self, is like the socket into which our life force is plugged. It links us to the Infinite, and when it decides to quit the body to reunite with Source, our physical life is extinguished. The power, however, simply changes its focus.

This book is concerned with an aspect of self-awareness, accessible to us, by way of astrology and the twelve Sun signs. It is also concerned with relationship, because we cannot know ourselves in the absence of relationship. Both are portals to the Infinite.

Soul-mate relationships evoke particularly powerful dynamics that penetrate to the heart of what we are about here. They link us soul-to-soul with another, and in so doing they awaken us to aspects of ourselves we never knew existed. And lest you labor under the illusion that a soul-mate relationship will mean the end of all your problems and the beginning of a life of perpetual bliss, here are some words from a wise old soul, when counseling a young woman newly in love: "Yes, you do indeed have a soul-mate connection. And soul mates can end up killing each other!"

A little dramatic perhaps. But the message is clear: soul-mate relationships are not always easy! This book will tell you why.

Some see astrology as an interesting amusement, an aside to the serious business of life—having no real value other than entertainment. This book is an invitation to look at astrology in a new way. Astrology is one of the most profound knowledge systems and intuitive arts on the planet. It seamlessly blends cosmology, philosophy, and sacred psychology. It was the father of astronomy. Eons ago, when people looked heavenward and observed the patterns of the stars, they observed how these patterns were reflected in the emotions and patterns of human behavior. As above, so below; celestial and terrestrial events were correlated. Furthermore, the ancients understood that the universe was *ensouled*. Many people today have lost that understanding. This book invites you to make your way back to the ancient knowing that still runs through you.

You are living and breathing your star map, your cosmic blueprint—your astrology—every second of every day. You walk it, you talk it, you think it—or it thinks you—whether or not you believe in it. Astrology is a portal, an access route, to higher consciousness.

The times in which we find ourselves living are pressuring us, like never before, to grow our consciousness—to open up to the truth of who we are. They are demanding we do so, and they will ensure we continue to do so, due to a breakdown of much that we know and love in the world of form. This demand is an evolutionary impulse, an evolutionary imperative, designed to steer us back home.

The sky on a clear night, its star-studded vastness stretching to infinity, is an external version of who and what we are on the inside. Our interior landscape, our mental and emotional patterning, is mirrored in the heavens.

We can touch the Infinite in ourselves by feeling our resonance with the stars and the cosmos, and by learning how their vibrations affect our psychology, our physiology, and our spirituality. And when we touch the Infinite, we touch home.

The View from Above

The cosmos is a vast living body,
of which we are still parts.
The sun is a great heart
whose tremors run through our smallest veins.
The moon is a great gleaming nerve-centre
from which we quiver forever.
Who knows the power that Saturn has over us,
or Venus?
But it is a vital power,
rippling exquisitely through us
all the time.
—D. H. Lawrence

Ｗe are living in an era of dramatically accelerating consciousness. The discoveries that scientists are making and have made in the past decade lead us to the undeniable conclusion that we exist in a field of consciousness that is ineffably, mysteriously Infinite.

This field has been called *the Mind of God, the matrix, the web,* and in earlier days of scientific exploration, *the etheric.* The field embraces everything in the known universe: the cosmos (the word itself means "order"), our planet, and every creature on our planet and in the invisible universe. Science and spirit, after their lengthy estrangement, are coming together, and the field of consciousness is where they are meeting. On the scientific side of the equation, we are being shown that there is a single, unified field, connected on levels of which we are not aware. The evidence is clear: something that was once connected to something else will always remain connected—whether a photon, a strand of DNA, or a person. We are no longer observers in this field; discoveries in quantum physics have demonstrated that we are participants, because everything in the field is linked. The observer is an integral part of the world he observes.

Mystics and wise ones have known this truth for as long as people have walked the planet: we are all One. Quantum physics and mysticism are telling us the same thing. Finally, modern science has come of age and is in agreement with ancient wisdom. The universe is an ordered field of energetic vibration—and it is permeated by consciousness.

Mainstream science may not yet go so far as to say there is an intelligence in the universe that knows itself, is aware, and is one soul—but those ahead of the game (past and present) would.

The physical world, the world of form in which we live, is one huge hologram—where every part contains the whole. It is an illusion, a dream world, a computer program, this hologram we call 3-D "reality." (Whose reality is it?) And here we find ourselves.

There is not much we can do about the reality we find ourselves participating in. We can however, change how we participate in it, through realizing the infinite consciousness that we are. The truth is that we are individual forms expressing the formless. We are infinite beings in finite bodies. Through consciousness, we can access the deep infinity of the universe.

If we remain "unconscious" (that is, unawakened), our lives are lived on the surface, on the level of the physical. We are unable to imbue our lives with the meaning derived from a sense of our immortality. We do not touch the Infinite.

In his book *Life After Death*, Deepak Chopra writes:

> *[T]he ability of consciousness to shape our lives is the most permanent thing about us, the one aspect of the mind we can expect to continue.*[1]

Now, not only do we know that we can affect the field, and the field in turn affects us, but we are also hearing that consciousness is permanent. In other words, that aspect of ourselves that is conscious cannot be extinguished. Consciousness cannot be destroyed. We are consciousness riding in a physical body; our survival beyond physical death is therefore a certainty.

The ego—source of our pain

While we are here, in the world of form, it is the ego that tends to dominate consciousness. The ego's job is to keep us alive in our physical separateness, and in doing so, it gives rise to a separate self that believes it must fight and compete for its survival. This is the material world, where ego is the defining feature.

The ego overidentifies with the mind and obscures the pure consciousness that is the real, or higher, self. This process creates pain and fear, arising out of the belief that we are separate and alone in the world. This ego-orientation is a manifestation of the "yang" focus that has dominated Western culture for thousands of years. We are at a critical stage in our evolution where the need is to become more "yin," which is to say, less materialistic and more receptive to natural law. This time is urgently upon us.

The pain we feel as a consequence of this ego-orientation maintains a sense of abandonment and separateness. It is a vicious circle because the more fear we feel, the more we try to escape from it with our minds. We think that if we have more of what the world offers that we like, and less of what it gives us that we don't like, we will stop the pain. But our minds cannot free us from fear. Only releasing ourselves from the mind, with its endless procession of thought forms, can we come back to infinite love and the awareness of our connection with the whole universe, which is who we really are.

The ways of the ego are powerful, and the pull to be completely enmeshed and identified with the body is a strong one. Most people are in fact centered in their egos rather than in their souls. The "consensus or herd state" (the mainstream of society—around 75 percent of the population) belongs to this group. These people do not question what their society tells them to do or think. Their beliefs are conditioned by the prescriptions of society. The leaders in society belong to this group—having spent some time in former lives climbing to the top of it. When one is centered in the ego, the voice of the soul (intuition or knowing) is at best a background whisper.

Living an ego-centered existence can be satisfying for a time. The ways of the world are often an intoxicating distraction. But the day of reckoning inevitably arrives. Ego-based desires and choices lead to separateness—and ultimately pain. Essentially, living in the ego lowers our vibratory rate, which takes us further into fear. We've heard it said many times—there are two emotions, love and fear. In fact, love is not an emotion. It is our original, pure state. Love is not of this world. It comes into this world from the formless, infinite side of the veil.

When we become captured by the duality of the world of form, we enter into the territory of fear, pain, and anxiety, because these are the emotions that maintain the polarized vibrations responsible for physical forms. The negative emotional states (which are where the ego tries to keep us) have a low vibratory rate; the lower we vibrate, the more susceptible we are to the negativity in the world around us. We become more susceptible to ill health and disease, and our life situation (interpersonal relationships, finances, career) deteriorates.

We all have the power within us to reverse this trend and to wake up to the truth of who we are, and to feel, in our everyday lives, the silent but very real presence of the soul. This has the effect of raising our vibratory frequency and spinning us into a state of Oneness, which is our authentic state. Thoughts keep us anchored in duality, but conscious awareness of our thinking gives us the power to move beyond it. This is the reason meditation has been a favored pathway of the spiritual aspirant.

We are infinite beings in an infinite universe. And it is the soul within us, operating beyond the bounds of conventional (or unawakened) consciousness, that offers us the possibility of living an ego-free existence.

Service to selves

The cancer cell is a good example of the ego's effect on a micro level. In putting its own survival first, ahead of the good of the whole, the cancer cell ultimately destroys both itself and its host. The cancer cell feels itself to be separate and apart from the rest of the body. Something similar is going on in our world on a larger scale. When individual, short-term needs and desires (lack of consciousness) are prioritized over the good of the collective (higher consciousness), we see the repercussions on the planet (our host)—i.e., natural disasters and climatic disturbances. Individual desires (desires are always separatist) also gravitate to identification with a particular group—defined by race, religion, or some other commonality. We then see the "us versus them" phenomenon: the reason for the conflict and division, the atrocities and crimes committed by man against his fellow man, and the story of our history on this planet. The division of self against others creates devastation both on a personal level and on a collective level.

This "service to self" is the domain of the ego. When we are centered in the vastness of our infinite selves, we take care of ourselves, our bodies, and our life situation—but we carry the awareness that we are part of the whole. Service to others is a natural outflow of this awareness.

In this madness we call the world, the soul's needs are often sacrificed by ego consciousness, in its quest to secure its survival.

As astrologer Steven Forrest says, "Earth is not the most prestigious address in the galaxy, and the fact we're here means we're all a little crazy."

We certainly are. We need only look at our history through the twentieth century to see that. And are we getting it? Are we realizing where "service to self" is taking us? All around us we see the evidence piling up, of the consequences of this orientation: the ego's me-first, competitive, and insecure striving for a safe place in a material world. Leaving aside our heinous history of bloodshed and violence, on another level entirely our culture's preoccupation with trivia and celebrity hype; its obsessive concern with appearance, health, wealth, status, anti-aging, and image; and the endless laws and regulations that prevent us from taking responsibility for ourselves all remind us that we are living in a society where ego rules. These are all distractions the ego employs to convince us the world is a fearful place, where we must compete and be beautiful, rich, and successful to survive. And life is dangerous! We must secure our place in it—quickly, before we die.

Of course, aging reminds us that date isn't so far away, so we must try to retain our youthfulness in an attempt to hide that truth from ourselves and others. In our adherence (based on primal security fears) to the ego's agenda, we effectively shut out the soul. And this is always to our detriment—and to the detriment of the collective and the planet, as we are discovering.

When we shut out our soul, we close off our link to the Infinite and distance ourselves from the all-encompassing source of nurturance and love, and from our awareness of the plan and purpose for our lives.

Love, which is not innately of this world, can enter in only when we are open to infinite consciousness. The ego keeps the focus on the world of form, and love is easily mangled here. Love is abused and misused with an overlay of the ego's fearfulness. It becomes no longer recognizable as love. It feels precarious to use the word at all.

When we can detach from the world of form and remain in the presence of our infinite consciousness, life miraculously transforms. Love, or the sacred in us, flowers.

The language of the Infinite

The Infinite speaks to us in the language of symbol and metaphor, dreams, promptings, moods, feelings. If we pay attention, the clues it leaves are all around us.

We can all access these clues the formless offers us. When we do, we know ourselves more deeply, in our wakened as well as our unconscious aspects. Our lives have greater depth and greater meaning. And our relationships are correspondingly richer, deeper, and more fulfilling.

This book is my invitation to you to do just that: to enter into the deeper meaning of your psychic make-up, and in doing so, to come to know yourself as the infinite consciousness you are.

Inscribed over the temple of Apollo at Delphi was the phrase *Know Thyself.* The ancients knew that unraveling the mystery of who we are, and of this life we find ourselves living, is what we are about here. One thing is certain, we will not go there—into the mystery and into the soul—if we listen only to the ego, if we reside exclusively in the world of form.

The mystery that is the Infinite cannot be accessed through the "normal" (i.e., mind-dominated) state of awareness. It can only be approached through symbols and higher states of consciousness. Symbols act as a bridge between the conscious and the unconscious. Astrology is a symbolic language. It is a language that has been around for thousands of years, and it is currently experiencing a renaissance. This resurgence of interest in astrology has come about for good reason.

The reason is that we have become alienated from our inner selves, from our souls, as our culture and society have compelled us to live horizontal, rather than vertical, lives. We have lost connection with our inner awareness, and we have given away our power to outer authorities. Feeling the pull of our souls—of the vertical, multilayered aspects of our being—we are searching for lives of meaning amid the superficiality and emptiness of modern life. We are feeling the pull toward a more "yin" way of being, away from the "yang" culture we have been born into—where materialism, competition, and aggression dominate. Astrology is yin; it is receptive, symbolic, and capable of bringing an awareness of the cyclic and ordered patterning of natural law.

We are attempting to live a symbolic life whether we are aware of it or not: witness the fascination with celebrities' lives, for example, our latter-day gods and goddesses. These individuals are symbols of ancient archetypal energies, Aphrodite or Venus, Apollo, Diana . . . and are clues to the energies we crave to connect with. But to embrace the symbolic life consciously means we bring meaning to our own journeys, we invite the mystery into our own lives. We stop living vicariously through others and live for ourselves, guided by the wisdom of our deepest knowing.

Here is the reason astrology is being rediscovered and has evolved to merge with depth psychology: the symbolic language of the stars has the power to connect us with the deepest parts of our being. This is because it touches our souls and silently acknowledges their importance in our outer lives. The linkage astrology makes between our inner lives and the planets places us in our rightful context, as cosmic beings. Astrology recognizes the truth of "as above, so below"—that celestial events are reflected in terrestrial ones.

The soul is the interface between both of those levels. It links our personality self with our infinite self. The truth is, we live from the inside out. Everything we act out, or that comes to us from the outer world, has its birthplace in the home of the invisible.

The soul is an emissary from the Mind of God. If we fail to hear the voice of the soul, if we do not listen to the knowing within and listen instead to the hollow imperatives of society, our parents, our partners—and worse, our own egos—we betray ourselves, and our lives become fractured, empty, painful, stagnant. We become alienated from our true being. This is the true meaning of the word *tragedy*.

So this is the quest each of us will ultimately follow—to know ourselves. And it is hardly a simple task. It is a journey that, if we are open to it, will engage and challenge us for a lifetime.

There are many layers that make up the conscious and the unconscious. The forces of our collective history and our personal history, as they play out in compensatory behaviors, are quite resistant to being examined, brought to the light of day (or the light of consciousness), and released. It takes drive, courage, and insight to become conscious of our old patterns, programming, and cultural conditioning. But this is the way to live a truly meaningful life. To live with meaning requires the richness and depth of a connection to the different dimensions of life. The symbolism of astrology can take us into those dimensions.

The new astrology is called *evolutionary astrology*. It gives symbolism and metaphor pride of place in connecting us with the Infinite. It is a way to step off the mind-numbing treadmill of a life lived through unconscious pattern repetition and the dictates of the infantile ego, and an invitation to embrace a larger sense of being. When we become aware of our evolution through astrology, we become aware of ourselves as spiritual beings. Ego no longer dominates; we become spacious.

If we want to grow old with beauty, dignity, ease of body, and largeness of spirit, then it is time to look beyond the package that we see in the mirror and discover the truth: we are part of infinite consciousness—and we are always connected to it. We are always connected to the source of unlimited love. When we lose ourselves in our personalities, we forget that before we were physical beings, we were formless spiritual beings. Beneath the surface, this is still who we are. Our relationship with spirit and with the mystery never really went away. We just forgot it was there.

Jungian psychologist James Hollis eloquently describes the journey in this way:

> *The greatest gift of depth psychology is returning to us again the possibility of a deep dialogue with this mystery. We are all susceptible to being bewitched by surfaces, but the energy that moves the whirling constellations, that moved the great myths, and moved our ancestors, still moves within you.*[2]

Consciousness created us and everything in the visible and invisible universe. This is the Mind of God, and this is the mystery. We live in it, and we are aspects of it. We have the power to create, just as the Source does. We are in fact always creating—and we are doing it either consciously or unconsciously. If we create unconsciously, we eventually experience pain and contraction. If we create con-sciously, we inevitably experience bliss and expansion.

If you want bliss and expansion, rather than pain and contrac-tion, the question to ask yourself is this: *Do I have a relationship with the Infinite?* Without such a relationship, all human relation-ships become an arena for ego games. Deep, soul-centered relation-ships always grow and evolve within limitless consciousness. They recognize, however silently, the presence of the sacred amidst their daily pleasures and pains.

The world we see is but a reflection of who we are and what we believe. It is a construction of the mind. Our mission is to discover who we are, really. Who is this eternal soul living through the flesh and blood of a fleeting existence on a relatively small planet some-where in the Milky Way galaxy? Who is behind the eyes that look out and observe the world? Once we see who we are, we uncover a greater level of compassion for ourselves—and for others. We are all walking a hard road. Our reality then changes, because our awareness has shifted.

And the world outside looks different from then on. It is no longer random, meaningless. It becomes more benign, kinder, friendlier, the outer a reflection of the inner. And reality, we then discover, is, and always was, an inside job.

The Vibratory Dance
of the Cosmos

Love nothing
but that which comes
to you woven in the pattern of your destiny.
For what could more aptly fit your needs?
—Marcus Aurelius

Spiritual traditions talk of "coming home" after we die—meaning that we return to the place we started out from. Everything in the physical universe begins in the invisible. It falls into form, and at the end of its life on Earth, falls back out. Back to the invisible, back to pure consciousness, back to the mystery from which it came.

Eventually, somewhere on the long journey through form, we wake up to the reality that we are not just physical beings living lives of pain and loss, with a few short-lived pleasures along the way. We come to know through the deepening of our consciousness that we are, in fact, eternal creatures of the cosmos.

There are many ways to become more conscious. If all else fails, life itself will make us wake up. Repeated pain and the emotional wounds of unconscious choices eventually erode resistance and penetrate to the soul. After being beaten up by life, we finally become aware how some of our choices have brought us pain. This is the slow way—albeit a popular one.

Another way is through portals like astrology that provide a gateway or a link between the inner and the outer, the mundane world and the soul. These enable us to give meaning to the events of our lives. Astrology has been given a bad press since the scientific paradigm overtook the formerly held knowledge that the universe was ensouled.

Magazine and newspaper horoscopes are the closest most people ever come to astrology. Predictions based on the Sun signs are too generalized to be anything other than a superficial, if somewhat intriguing, entertainment.

Astrology doesn't need you to believe in it. It happens regardless. Your character, your life circumstances, the events you attract, the people you attract—these are all reflections of your astrological make-up. And you have been given exactly what you need for this life. As above, so below; the microcosm is a reflection of the macrocosm. It was Carl Jung, the great pioneer of depth psychology and believer in the power of astrology, who coined the word *synchronicity*—the basis on which our understanding of astrology rests. Whatever is occurring in the wider cosmos is simultaneously reflected down through the levels to the microcosm. And those levels are indeed multifaceted—ranging from the density of the physical (events in the world) to the subtlety of the emotional (psycho-spiritual states). Thus we see, for example, that a transit of Saturn can bring physical obstacles that block our progress in the world, equally as readily as it can signify a time of depression and anxiety.

Jung further observed that what we do not become conscious of inwardly, will come to us from outside as fate. Astrology is a knowledge system that seamlessly unites the inner being with the outer, the unconscious with the conscious, character with fate.

It is a way to become conscious of what is occurring inwardly.

So what, then, are Sun signs? The zodiacal belt in the heavens is composed of twelve signs—representative of universal life principles. The Sun travels through the thirty degrees of each of the zodiacal signs in one calendar year. Our Sun sign is the sign the Sun occupied at the time of our birth. The essence, or principles, of that particular sign is the essence we need, as individuals, to feed the solar function in our psyche.

The solar function is how we express our individuality, how we consciously seek validation. It is the essence we radiate. If we want to feel alive and vital each day, to be an active player in the game of life, then we need to feed our inner Sun by honoring the principles of our Sun sign. The signs represent twelve life principles or truths. These are universal principles that one by one unfold or evolve— from the Arian principles of new beginnings, birth, and survival, through to the Piscean truths of surrender, release, and the death of form. In between, every facet of life is described by, and assigned to, a particular zodiacal sign.

If you feed the solar function (and in this book I will explain what that is for each of the signs), then you will experience higher levels of emotional wellness and engagement in your life! You'll have more fun, feel more alive and more centered. And what's more, your relationships will flow with greater ease—when you meet your own needs to *be* Aries, or Scorpio, or Capricorn; when you walk in the world as the being you came in to be—*and* when you acknowledge your partner's need to be their Sun too! The life force flows within you when you tune in to the energetic wave of your Sun sign.

Predictive astrology, fate, and free will

Predictions based on Sun signs are not where astrology's greatest gifts and truths lie. Astrology is not (or shouldn't be) used as a predictive tool. This is not the type of astrology to which evolutionary astrologers subscribe. We are more concerned with helping our clients understand their natures, strengths, challenges, and karmic patterns. Part of this may involve looking ahead to the various waves of energy that will be surging in on the cosmic tide in the future. But this is purely in order to help our clients align themselves with the purposes and intentions of the "soul lessons" coming their way, and not to help them avoid these lessons!

There are around three hundred million different biochemical activities happening in our bodies every second. How does the body coordinate all of this? Even more mind-boggling, the body is also, at the same time, monitoring the movement of the stars. Circadian, lunar, and seasonal cycles impact our biology. The stupendous intelligence required to organize all of that must surely have an awareness of the microcosm and the macrocosm, the intracellular and the interstellar. If it didn't, this level of coordination would be impossible. Where is this intelligence? Is it in our bodies, or is it in the stars? Or is it in both?

The pattern of the stars at the moment of our first breath is the pattern, or the blueprint, for our life. Our destiny is woven in this pattern—known as the birth chart. The birth chart is a map of the earthly life of a divine being. But the map is not the territory. It is a symbolic representation of the story we have brought in with us, and the story our life may become. Symbolism means experiencing the spiritual level through the mundane—the planets are the mundane (denser) aspect of spiritual, or higher frequency, energies.

The chart is a map of our personality and our potential. It is the story we are bringing to life, through the living of it. It is our choice either to accept our story, our fate—with its inherent limitations, challenges, gifts, and strengths (the "themes" depicted in the birth chart)—and use it to create a conscious life, or to rail against it.

Our fate is unique to us. We created it—or it was created for us—in perfect accordance with our karma and the universe's intentions for us. The soul designed the vehicle of our personality, from behind the scenes. Or was it the Mind of God that decided what we needed to learn in this life, which star map would serve us best? The driving force is beyond this personality and this world of five-sensory, three-dimensional "reality." We do need to know this much, though: we are all given precisely what we need for the journey.

There *is* a purposeful, conscious plan for our lives; we did not come in as blank slates. That purpose was sketched in the Infinite and encoded into our DNA. DNA is a physical and vibratory thread of the mental and emotional patterning that determines our life in the world of form. At the moment of the first breath, the individual begins his or her physical life. As the lungs inhale for the first time and numerous biological systems kick into action, the DNA, which has pre-recorded the child's genetic inheritance, registers the vibratory frequency of the cosmos at that particular time and in that particular location on the planet. The miracle of the physical birth is but one of the miracles of new life.

Everything in the universe is composed of vibration. The physical is the slowest, most dense vibration. But we are not composed of physical matter only. The soul that uses the body as its vehicle has its own vibratory rate. It chose a certain moment in time to makes its entrance, because the vibratory frequency exactly corresponded to that which the soul needed for this life. Put another way, the universe had a need for the energy of the cosmos, at a particular moment in time, to be embodied in us!

The Greek word *hora*, from which the word *horoscope* comes, means the "correct moment." So our ancestors understood that our moment of birth (symbolized in our horoscope) was the *right* one for us to be born in. Thus we are unique not only in terms of our genetic inheritance, but more significantly than we may realize, in terms of the vibratory frequency that dances within our DNA.

The quality of a time, in terms of its vibratory or energetic resonance, is imprinted onto whatever is being birthed, or coming into existence at that moment. That imprint is there forever after. This applies to all new beginnings, such as the first meeting of a couple who are destined to become lovers. The motif of that moment of the first meeting will be carried with them throughout the course of their relationship, and it is highly significant.

The vibratory pattern can be read or interpreted through the symbolism of the chart. We can no more alter the pattern of our birth charts than we can fly unaided to the Moon. We are stuck with it. The horoscope is a map of character—and therefore a map of destiny. It is the map that was deemed "right" for each of us. Fate is character unfolded in time. However, it would be a mistake to think that the pattern depicted in the birth chart was a static thing, or that we had no choice as to how it would be played out. The chart is bursting with potential, and every piece of the symbolism has the capacity to be expressed in a lower way or a higher one. It is an evolving depiction of our character as we move through the various phases of the life cycle. Our free will determines how we mold and refine that character.

Fate or free will—which is it?

The truth, as with all good truths, is a paradox. Both fate and free will operate simultaneously throughout our lives; they coexist. The clue to understanding the paradox lies in the word *will*. Using our will, we can either align ourselves with our fate—which is our divine pattern—or pull against it. In aligning ourselves with our destiny, our will and the will of the divine are united—and with that acceptance comes freedom. If we fail to exercise our will, and live unconsciously, then what comes to us appears to be out of our hands, to be truly fated.

In other words, if we release our attachment to how we think our lives should be, and instead accept them as they are (there are always limitations in the world of form!), we become "free." It was Voltaire who said that each of us is free at the moment we choose to be. Ultimately, the soul is the driver; we have less control than we believe—so when we accept our unique path and relax into life, life rewards us, and everything we need comes, most mysteriously, into our lives.

One of the values of astrology lies in its ability to depict and anticipate the cycles, or energetic waves, that mark our evolutionary journey through life. And by interpreting the symbolism, we can better understand their intent. We have an opportunity to align the conscious with the unconscious. The intent is a mechanism for the evolution, or ascension, of our consciousness. We can then view the phases of life, the various turns of the wheel of fortune, through more enlightened eyes. Knowing we have the ability to bring consciousness to these cycles of life, we can honor the meaning they have for us by flowing with them, rather than resisting them. Pain is always about resistance. Resistance is yang, receptiveness is yin. The cosmic tide has turned and we are, like it or not, being urged toward a yin way of being.

There is a purpose for the hard times and difficulties we experience in our lives, as well as the heart-opening moments we each encounter. They are part of the ebb and flow, the rhythm and the dance that is life. Subtly, and often not so, these difficulties are initiating us into an awareness of the nature of life itself. And in the end, there are no mistakes and nothing is ever wasted.

In addition to our individual life cycles, our planet, too, is living through cycles, or epochs. Through the ancient knowledge system of astrology, we know about the twelve ages or twelve epochs that humanity needs to live through to learn the mysteries of the self. Each epoch corresponds to the twelve signs of the zodiac. It is fascinating to read prophecies from ages past that describe the transition of the ages from Pisces to Aquarius. We are currently living in the earliest days of the Aquarian age.

Many of these prophecies speak of the boundaries between religion and science disappearing, as people discover that everything, matter included, is a wave. The only difference between spirit and matter is one of frequency. Everything is, at heart, wave-like. And aptly, the symbol for Aquarius is a supernal being pouring waves from his open-ended (infinite) pitcher.

Karma is a universal law and a primary mechanism of evolution. It is a balancing process through which we experience consequences of thoughts and deeds. Thoughts that have been held consistently (through many lifetimes) gather power, and they form the beliefs that create our reality. Karma is, in a sense, crystallized thought. The "beliefs" depicted in the birth chart are the consequence of thought. We take these beliefs to be real, to reflect the "world." In fact, they have no reality outside of our own experience. We create it all. The world of thought is endlessly creative, and whatever we hold on to (old insecurities and fears as well as positive beliefs) has the power to mold external reality.

In this way, the outer and the inner are reflections of each other. We attract to us the circumstances and people we do, throughout our lives, through karmic necessity. Like attracts like. This is the Law of Attraction. Our birth charts depict that karma—as well as the intent, or purpose of the life we have just entered into. The intent is the soul's evolutionary desire to transcend the limitations of "erroneous" belief. In other words, it is helping us to heal—or make ourselves whole.

For many of us, freeing ourselves from the limitations of our thought patterns, which originated beyond this lifetime and were "confirmed" for us by the events and experiences of this one, is not an easy task. Conscious awareness is needed to break the patterns, or they will be repeated. Our life design is unique and, mysteriously, multilayered. It can be played out in a higher expression or a lower one. The difference in evolutionary levels is the difference between living a life immersed in the pain of the world and living with an awareness of the sacred, infinite dimension that orchestrates all.

The beautiful thing is that the universe needed us to be exactly who we are—to embody the sky pattern of the moment of our birth. Our pattern is unique to us (which is why DNA testing is used in identification—that pattern, the hologram, is there within every cell of our bodies). It needed us to come into this dimension and live out life in the physical—as infinite beings in resonance with the music of the cosmos. Perhaps this is how the Mind of God knows itself. Just as we cannot know ourselves in isolation (without relationship), the creative force, the Supreme Being, God, needs to know itself through its relationships with its creations.

As we live out our destiny, we fulfill the purpose of our incarnation—which was, and is, simply to be *who we are!* To be who and what our higher self decreed we needed to be in order to manifest the spark of the Infinite within, to express our uniqueness through the creative act of living our lives. Our higher self, or soul, set us off on this life with the intention also of helping us heal the wounds and the karmic patterns, accumulated through countless lives, that have brought us such pain. It is always there to help and guide us toward this healing. The people we meet, and those we form intimate relationships with, have come into our lives through design. There are no accidents. All is in aid of our evolution and growth toward wholeness.

It seems it is impossible to become more conscious and thus more blissful and expansive, whole and healed, unless we are willing to turn inward and away from the world. We need to listen to the language the soul speaks—through the clues it leaves—and to go more deeply into our own lives. Life on the surface, where the majority of people reside these days, is bereft of meaning because the surface is not where the soul is to be found.

The dream world we mistake for reality

Marcus Aurelius said, "Love nothing but that which comes to you woven in the pattern of your destiny. For what could more aptly fit your needs?" We do not know what our real needs are, because we are living in a dream world; we are immersed in an illusion, the illusion of 3-D. Our vision is narrow, our senses limited. The matter we observe—even with instruments, is only 0.5 percent of all calculated mass. What we see with our eyes alone is much less.[1] That means we're pretty much blind to most of what is going on here. But something, somewhere, is not. From a larger perspective, everything that comes to us has a purpose and an intention. This purpose is the one we need. We do not need to find our purpose. If we trust the Infinite, our soul within, it will find us.

> *To the extent that the ruling heavens favor your beginnings and further life, you will pursue the promise of your birth; especially if Plato is correct, and antiquity with him,*

in saying that when anyone is born they are given a certain daimon, a life-guardian—destined by one's very own star.[2]
—Marsilio Ficino, 1489

When we use our "free will" to align ourselves with our destiny, we uncover the biggest secret. The secret is that life is really very simple when we give up the need to control it. Peace and freedom can be ours when we remember this.

Aligning ourselves with our destiny, or our cosmic inheritance, has more benefits; it has the power to connect us with the Now moment. Maintaining this alignment with the Now requires a level of mental self-discipline, but the ironic thing is this discipline is effortless; it is much simpler than it first appears. And that is a paradox for the higher-minded to contemplate. It is effortless effort—known as *wu wei* in Taoism.

Because of the density of the physical dimension, there are natural laws that we are compelled to abide by. We have no choice. Understanding and honoring these natural laws means we bring a level of discipline or order, or control if you like, to our physical lives. The mind is no different. Thoughts are less dense than physical bodies, but are still subject to these laws. We know this because we can attract events in the material world through our thinking. Thinking is creative, and therefore it is a force in the material world, subject to the universal laws of the material plane.

The root of most of our ills is found in wrong-thinking; but the secret reminds us that all we need to do is step off the merry-go-round of endless self-talk—usually negative (mind is ego's domain) and relax into the Now moment. This decision aligns us with our destiny, and through this comes peace and freedom. All that is required is an acceptance of what is (opening the heart) and the peaceful, effortless discipline of quieting the mind. It was Pythagoras who said that no man is free who cannot command himself.

Aligning ourselves with our soul's intention for this lifetime is a process of gradual unfolding of our awareness of who we are, from the inside out. Practicing a moment-to-moment conscious connection with whatever is occurring, and acceptance of it, is an exercise in opening the heart and silencing the ego.

Astrology can help us to gain clarity, to step up the unfolding of that awareness. It helps us to see our soul's intentions and to become more conscious through this understanding.

In the absence of a complete birth chart (which tells the story of life in astonishing detail), the Sun sign alone gives us valuable gems of information—it tells us what we need to do to be fully alive; what make of engine is driving us this time around; what we need to do to be authentic, to be fully functioning, to be sane. How we can feed the Sun, the "*soul*-ar function" in our psyche, is how we live in total engagement with life.

Obviously we don't need a knowledge of astrology. People have lived very successfully on the planet without this knowledge since the beginning of time. But in days past, people were more in tune with the natural laws and the cosmic ordering of life. We now need to consciously seek this understanding because, quite honestly, we don't seem to be getting it right anymore. There are many tools or guidelines available to help us, and astrology is one such tool.

It is necessary to realize that learning about ourselves through astrology doesn't take away the need for experience (that would be futile)—life was designed to be an experiential exercise. Experiences are necessary, and if we try to avoid them, we miss the point. Astrology's greatest gift lies in its ability to put us in touch with ourselves in a way that illustrates (symbolically) our inner experience and our outer life—the events and the feelings, the content and the form. When we understand ourselves on the inner level, we intuit our life's purpose. Then we can choose to accept and work with it, or not—freedom, or not. The choice is ours.

We need astrology because we are not in touch with ourselves.
If we were whole, we would not need a doctor. If we were in
a state of being, of Tao, or grace, we would not need astrology.
Astrology, used correctly, can help people to be in this state.[3]
—Gregory Szanto

This book is a journey through the Sun signs from a relational perspective. The Sun in the birth chart is a powerful symbol because everything is filtered, at a conscious level, through the Sun. Feeding our Sun, by following the needs and drives of the principles of the sign our Sun falls in, gives us a "sunny disposition." We have vitality, and we are engaged in life with all our heart and soul. And only when we are fully engaged in life are we deserving of the gift of deep and meaningful relationships. And only then can love flourish.

Listening to the message of your Sun sign, your *soul*-ar power, vitalizes your spirit and nurtures your soul, strengthening your link with the Infinite. Your inner Sun is an encapsulation of your life's direction and energy. The Sun, in this solar system at least, is reflected through the signs of the zodiac as your Guiding Star.

3

The Light and Dark Sides
of the Sun Signs

*One does not become enlightened by
imagining figures of light,
but by making the darkness conscious.*
—Carl Jung

The zodiacal signs represent an ancient knowledge system, which sought to capture and describe the fundamental principles of life. It is a knowledge system that has evolved and is continually evolving. The principles the signs illuminate are alive in nature and within the psyche of every individual. All of life is there, somewhere within the twelvefold division of the zodiac. The signs contain everything we know in this mortal realm and some of what lies beyond it. There is the passion and sexuality of our deepest instinctual desire to merge, to transform and heal ourselves through merging (Scorpio and Pluto). There is the urge to make ourselves secure, to take responsibility, to perfect ourselves, to be disciplined, and to work toward achieving something significant (Capricorn and Saturn). There is the desire to connect with others, to attract and be attractive, to relate, to calm the waters of conflict, and to be fair and balanced (Libra and Venus). There is the craving to connect with something higher—the divine discontent that compels us to transcend, or escape, the restrictions of mundane life and dance, create, drink wine, or dissolve into a movie or a novel (Pisces and Neptune). Anything you can think of has its representation in one or another of the twelve zodiacal signs and their planetary agents.

We all have the twelve zodiacal signs, or the energies they represent, within us, and each one of the signs has its pros and cons, its light and its dark sides, its cop and its criminal. They are all components, with their potentials and pitfalls, of our psychic make-up. So we are not "one sign," our Sun sign. We are all twelve signs—to lesser or greater degrees (depending on their emphasis in our own charts). All twelve principles of life make up the human psyche.

But the Sun! Let's talk about the Sun. The Sun is what gives us life. It is our star in this corner of the universe, and it sustains us—physically and spiritually. Our Sun sign is much more than a description of a collection of character traits. It is the energy our soul is using, in this lifetime, to get us to where we're going. Our Sun sign is the power source for our individuality.

The Sun in our solar system is known esoterically as a transmitting station for spiritual frequencies (or consciousness) coming in from a central sun. It is a kind of interdimensional gateway for higher dimensions entering our system. Interestingly, an increase in solar flares over the past few years has corresponded exactly with increased world temperatures. Obvious, when you think about it, that the Sun would have something to do with the heating of the planet.

What is less obvious is what that means on the level of consciousness. Much around us is being stepped up. These frequencies the Sun is receiving are split and filtered, or refined through the various vibratory frequencies of the planets and the zodiacal signs. The truths of astrology, it pays to keep in mind, have long been repressed by those who have sought to control us through the condemnation and suppression of esoteric knowledge.

(Note that Christianity's roots are firmly in the ancient, Sun-worshipping, astrologically based religions of Babylon and ancient Egypt. Hence all our Christian festivals are actually astrological ones.)

Each sign has its own set of tools, and these are given to us to help us fulfill the intentions of our soul. When we wholeheartedly embrace our Sun sign, we feel a sense of aliveness and vitality; we feel authentic. Our journey in this life is designed to be channeled through outward or active expression in the world, described by our Sun sign. If we neglect to consciously make that expression, we do ourselves a disservice. People who fail to energize their Sun sign, who fail to consciously live out the principles of that sign, gradually "run out of gas." These are the people who are half dead while they're still in a body. To fully participate in the life our soul has elected to live, we need to feed our inner Suns. If we don't, if we give up too soon, we start to die. Our Sun sign is our heading for life; it is what stirs our blood and vitalizes our heart center. Our very life force depends on the frequency of our Sun sign being lived out through our personal dialogue with life.

The sign the Sun was in at the time of birth colors the personality because, like the Sun in the solar system, it coordinates everything else. It is the center of our own universe. In astrology the Sun is referred to as the "identity" or the "ego"—but in fact the entire chart is the identity. The Sun is symbolic of the principles we resonate most strongly with and identify with. They are the principles the Infinite "knew" we most needed to experience, or to learn about, in this life. When we neglect our Sun, we fail to be true to ourselves. We become inauthentic because we are not in tune with our hearts. Every sign has a dark side; when we lose connection with our center, with our heart, we slip toward the dark. But when we honor the principles of our Sun sign, when we fully live them through our creative dialogue with life, we have light and life; we have a sunny disposition, we are in alignment—personality with heart.

The vibratory frequency of our Sun sign was hard-wired into us at birth. For example, if your Sun is in Pisces, learning about different states of consciousness and a desire to unite with something "higher," something sacred and more refined, will be a part of what you need to experience in this life. You will need to dive into the ocean of universal consciousness on a regular basis (through some artistic or spiritual practice). If you fail to do so, something inside you will quietly die. That desire to unite with something more spiritual can slip into the dark side and shortcuts will be taken—most obviously through drugs and alcohol. But a more evolved or "lighter" Piscean Sun will touch the sacred dimension and bring through an awareness of it by way of art, music, dance, literature—some form of creativity, or through empathetic and compassionate merging with others. The more evolved Piscean will make time to nourish the soul through meditation, spending time in nature, contemplation, and immersion in the mystery.

The Moon in astrology is symbolic of our unconscious needs (our lunar nature, as differentiated from our solar nature), and its principles are at play behind the scenes. They enfold and embed themselves into the unconscious sponge that is our early childhood. Our experience of our mother or early caregiver is there, soaking through membranes of heart and soul—becoming the pattern that will define our emotional needs, our instinctual desires to nurture and be nurtured, throughout our lives. Our experiences of the care, the love, the nurturing we received—or didn't—are re-enacted in our adult lives through our relationships, and it is the lunar aspect of our psyche that is responsible. Early experience becomes part of the matrix that forms the take we have on the world and it is all there in the psyche: pictured, like an X-ray, in the birth chart.

We can see why the principles embodied in the signs of the zodiac and their planetary agents were called gods and goddesses by the ancients, who knew the power of these cosmic archetypes. What was out there in the heavens was reflected in here, in the psyche of man and woman. The universe is ensouled—soul lies within every natural form. The pattern of soul is depicted in the astrological map. It is a representation of a cosmic arrangement that, as was observed through the ages, became embodied and enacted in the life of the individual.

We are players in a game of life governed by natural law. When we become more conscious, the gifts of our astrological patterning help us to create lives of greater clarity, and our purpose mysteriously filters its way through to us. We feel a joy in living fully awake to the Infinite. When we are less conscious, our pattern will play itself out, often in a more negative, or shadow, manifestation, and the positive potential inherent in our make-up will be unrealized. If we bemoan our fate, it is because we do not understand the potential inherent within it. Every coarse and creviced rock, we discover, as we develop a relationship with the Infinite, is a diamond in the rough. Every hardship, difficulty, struggle, and pain is simply the layer covering our pure and pristine soul. Our work here is to make acquaintance with our soul and to live our lives in the highest expression of who we came here to be. We are here, in short, to make the unconscious conscious.

To achieve this, we need to silence the voice of the ego—which would have us live a horizontal existence—and listen to the inner voice of our higher self. The ways of the soul are not always the most comfortable. We will be challenged many times, and many times we will enter the swamplands where painful betrayals, losses, and life-altering changes will confront us and lead us to construct various defenses and protective mechanisms. Our challenge will be then to dismantle these through relinquishing our resistance. We will need to learn to break the patterns of crystallized thought and erroneous belief. And we will need to let go of our desperation to control—and relax into, and trust in, the bigger plan.

The ways of the soul are so often the opposite of the ways of the ego, with its emphasis on separateness, physical security, status, and appearance. But the inner journey of making acquaintance with the soul is the only one worth taking. Refusal to take it has consequences on every level of our existence—physical, emotional, spiritual. We run the risk of ending up spiritual vacuums; all the richness and depth of soul sucked out of us by the continuous struggle to survive, to accumulate—to keep ourselves, our health, and our relationships "safe." The soul knows there is no safety in this world of impermanence. The only real security is the security of knowing we are infinite consciousness—and therefore we are indestructible. Everything in the world is temporary and impermanent. The soul knows the comfort zone the ego (or the mind) constructs is the most dangerous place to stay. And it knows to embrace change, to move into new places and experiences, to leave people and relationships that suck the energy out of us, to change careers at midlife, to show courage in the face of adversity, to have honesty and integrity, to feel the fear and do it anyway—these are the choices we need to make in order to live truly meaningful lives. This is how we live when we listen to the voice of the soul. We follow the directives of our hearts ahead of those of the ego-dominated mind.

Becoming more conscious means listening to the soul speak— quietly as it does—through our feelings and our intuition (our "knowing"). It means renouncing thinking, because the mind is the vehicle of the ego. The mind is meant to be the servant of the soul, but so often in this chaotic world we live in, it is the other way around. We are mind-dominated, and so our inner knowing is crowded out.

The soul also speaks in the voice of the shadow, that side of ourselves we have split off and sent underground, into the unconscious. The shadow has a personal component, built around past pain (e.g., the mother who abandoned you as a child) and a collective component, the universal fears and taboos—aging, abandonment, death. Relationships are the perfect arena for the personal shadow to come out of hiding, because it is here we project our unacknowledged selves. This is a mechanism our psyche uses to "make our shadow known." We become conscious of our shadow, through our relationships. Relationships are in the service of the soul. They bring this unrecognized part of ourselves to our attention, which we need to do, because it takes energy to keep the shadow material where it is—locked away. We should give thanks for our relationships—even for all the unhappiness they are capable of bringing our way—because through them we can become more conscious.

Our task in our relationships is to remain as conscious as we possibly can. When we experience deep and painful feelings, there is the clue that we have some work to do. No one said it would be easy. But more often than not, those intense feelings are the very ones that stand at the gateway to greater awareness. They are messengers from the soul, trying to get our attention. Is it our security button that our partner has unconsciously pressed? If so, where does that come from? This life, our childhood? Or does it come from beyond this life? Many of our most intense "themes" have their origin in former existences, and we sense this when we feel ourselves experiencing surges of emotion that seem to be out of all proportion to the current situation. Here is the clue that this is a life theme we have come in to work on and heal. We only heal and transform ourselves through the work of consciousness. Once we know that this is our karmic pattern, we are able to release the charge of that pattern. It is challenging because achieving that awareness can be a long and rocky road. But once we have the awareness, once we realize the pattern is causing no one more pain than ourselves, we can make the decision to let go of it and respond in a more positive way.

Our personalities are composed of both light and dark, as we live in a universe of duality. For everything in the manifest, physical, conscious universe, there is an opposite in the invisible, unconscious universe. Each sign of the zodiac, being a basic principle of life, can make itself known anywhere on the continuum from positive to negative—light or dark, conscious or unconscious. Discovering the endpoint, or highest expression of the Sun in our birth sign, moves us toward the light. And it is this we will be exploring in this book.

Following on from an exploration of the light and the dark sides of the signs is a collection of Sun-sign reflections on the possibilities and potentials open to you, for expanding your awareness and migrating further toward the "spiritual," the light end of the continuum. In this way and armed with this knowledge, your Sun sign becomes a portal into the Infinite. Connecting with the intent of your sign, and using the symbols of your sign in the outer world, allows the soul to make itself known in your life. Living a symbolic life can help you avoid the confusion of a "life on the surface."

If we can see ourselves in a different way, entertain some new ideas, push a little wider some of those mental boundaries, who knows how big the world could become? How big was it all along? Once we open our eyes, we may just find out.

The Sun-sign descriptions are written with reference to a partner. Whether this partner is your soul mate or someone you have recently formed a relationship with, the intent is to raise your awareness—and thus your compassion and tolerance—toward the person you are relating with. Relationships, as we've seen, are one of life's primary tools to raise our consciousness, by putting us in touch with what was unconscious. Relationships are so important to us because through them we can access, if we are sufficiently awake, the bits of ourselves in need of healing. Nothing can heal the way love can. Love is in service of the soul. We cannot know ourselves in isolation—we need the lens of "the other" to see ourselves; and more beautifully, through union with the other, we come to experience the bliss of Oneness, the fusion of polarity, the ecstasy of total merging.

As well as being our greatest joy, bringing us our most profound gifts, relationships are also the first casualty of our unconscious history. So often we burden our relationships with our unconscious wounds, and in doing so put them in jeopardy. Accepting responsibility for ourselves, our own emotional needs and psychological development, is imperative and the most important thing we can do for our relationships. To do this, we need to go deep into our own hearts. We need to grow up and take responsibility for our own emotional and psychological well-being.

Sometimes it is easier to see aspects of our own character when they are seen through the eyes of another. If you are reading your own sign, you may become aware of how you appear to another, to your partner. At the same time, the objectivity of this approach will open the door to feeling greater sensitivity and compassion for the person you truly are. We often have difficulty being as kind to ourselves, as forgiving of ourselves, as we are to others. I offer in this book some suggestions for dealing with partners of each sign. Understanding the drives that underlie the behaviors of our partners can help us to depersonalize the hurt they may unconsciously inflict (if they were conscious, they wouldn't hurt us!). If we can achieve this, the sting of relationship wars dissolves, and partnerships become more benign. Love becomes a continuous presence rather than an intermittent visitor.

So often, it isn't about us; it's about what's going on in the other person's psyche—their unconscious drives to meet equally unconscious needs. Knowing this can be a relief, but knowing must be followed by action. The suggestions in this book, then, are intended as signposts—ideas to help you along the mystifying, exciting, and often treacherous road of relationship. All of it, remember, is in service of the soul. Ours and theirs.

> *The struggle for growth is not for us alone; it is not self-indulgent. It is our duty, and service, to those around us as well, for through such departures from the comfortable we bring a larger gift to them.*[1]
> —James Hollis

If you are not in a relationship, I hope this approach will not distract from the insights I am intending to convey. After all, relationships occupy only a part of our time here in this life. Our first commitment must always be to ourselves. And our journey, ultimately, is ours alone.

One more suggestion: if you know your Moon sign, or your partner's Moon sign, do read through this sign as well. Although the focus in this book is on Sun signs and the need to honor these principles to vitalize life, the Moon sign gives valuable clues to powerful, usually unconscious, emotional needs. And as we know, emotional needs are potent drivers of behavior. Learning about the Moon sign of your partner will offer you greater insight.

Let us take the journey now, through the signs. By the end of our sojourn in the stars, I hope you will feel a sense of recognition and compassion for the character you are, for the personality you are working with, and for the purpose (or an aspect of it) of your mission here on Earth—and likewise for your partner.

—————————————— *Aries* ——————————————

Aries the Light

Aries, the first sign of the zodiac, is a fire sign. It is the entry point of the newly incarnating soul, and it is hot, passionate, bursting to take on life and to survive. The soul here is beginning a new round, and like the "young soul" it symbolizes, it is poised and ready to leap into life—headfirst. Aries is learning about courage; this is the endpoint. Aries energy is primal, instinctive.

The life stage Aries corresponds to is the newborn. When we feel this new, young energy—ruled by Ares, the god of war—we feel Aries on a visceral level. It is raw, uninitiated, experiential, bold, willing, fearless. It comes from the heart, from instinct—so it is impulsive, eager to reach into life, hungry for life. The survival instinct is powerful: look at a newborn baby, totally wired to survive outside the womb—to cry, to be fed, to be taken care of—until it is capable of taking care of itself.

Taking care of itself is Aries' forte. He'll fight to survive. He'll pit himself against everything life confronts him with; he won't be beaten. He is courageous, energized, and passionate. He is also a bit of a baby. He wants his own way. Aries energy is "me first" energy. This soul is not here to put others first; it is here to take on life with courageous, passionate intensity.

Life with an Aries Sun partner is like a crazy ride, full of new beginnings and the excitement of the unexpected. Aries energy is supercharged, impulsive, outwardly focused. To be in partnership with Aries is to be in partnership with the life force itself. New excitements and adventures come from out of the blue; startling discoveries, impulsive journeys, and new beginnings make frequent visitations. The light side of Aries is a gift from the gods in more ways than one.

Aries is a mixture of irresistible innocence . . . and frustrating selfishness. The man or woman born under the sign of the ram is a child in a grown-up's body. No contrived sophistication necessary. Aries is as Aries is. This delightful creature is so full of life, boredom will not enter in. And if you are the partner of an Aries, being stuck in the old routine will not be part of the agenda—as long as your Aries remembers to include you in all the excitement. The ram is capable of such intense self-involvement that your inclusion is not necessarily a given.

There is an impetuous streak in every Aries. And since we're focusing on the light side—what is it that makes Aries' impetuousness so attractive, so invigorating? Essentially, it is the capacity to come straight from the heart. The lack of differentiation between self and other, and the lack of forethought, means when Aries are in love, they give their all—unstintingly, trustingly, generously. The spontaneity Aries brings to romance can be breathtaking, mindblowing, energizing, and compelling. There is no holding back in the expression of love when Aries' heart is engaged. They will be the first to call, the first to suggest a date, the first to bring flowers and gifts and tickets to fun things and distant destinations. (They'll also be the first to assert their independence, the first to start a fight . . .)

> *Look, I can dare to fall down, and look, I can get up, and look, I'm not too hurt to try again.*
> —Diana Michener

If you are in a relationship with an Aries, you'll need to learn to be as honest as your partner is. (You probably won't want to be quite as blunt!) Aries appreciates the no-nonsense, direct, straight-talking approach. No point in beating around the bush. Be warned: he may start up arguments just for the sake of it. Life with Aries is seen as one big competition—and Aries wants to win it. So give him a run for his money and then let it go. If he feels he's won, he'll be happy. Eating the odd humble pie is something anyone involved with an Aries has to learn to do sooner or later—if she wants to stay in the relationship, that is. It's either that or suffer the wounds of a battered ego. Usually it is much less messy to fight the good fight and, most importantly, to know when to stop. Aries has to win, so when it comes to fighting, he can be utterly ruthless and determined.

Aries' courage is second to none. This child of warlord Mars, the ruling planet of Aries, fights as instinctively as breathing. Innate fearlessness is the brightest of Aries' lights. Aries gives its native the ability to get up each time she falls. Nothing is impenetrable, no mountain too high, no challenge too great. Aries knows no limitations. Everything is possible. And when life knocks her down, she gets up and starts again—like a baby learning to walk. No defeat is taken so much to heart that it stops her trying again. The rest of the world looks on in admiration, wishing it had half of Aries' determination to succeed.

In relationship, Aries' courage means life is always exciting, with the movement of change and the willingness to take on the new. Your Aries lover can take you to the ends of the earth in the quest for exploration and adventure. His is a noble quest. It is the quest of a spirit who has arrived here on the planet with a mission to experience as much of life as possible—as fast as possible! Aries may appear self-centered, but his impulse is pure. It is the impulse to live life to its fullest—and to be free to do so. Such willingness takes courage, because it means stepping out of the safety of the comfort zone. Aries is not a natural inhabitant of the comfort zone. Staying in one doesn't conquer mountains, create business empires, or achieve sporting stardom. Comfort-zone living is the antithesis of freedom-loving Aries. And to Aries freedom equates with survival. Take away one, and the other feels threatened.

Aries is the first sign of the zodiac; being first, it wants to stay that way. There is a pure, raw determination in Aries to compete and to win. Ruler Mars confers on its natives an inborn ability to embrace life head-on. The head, incidentally, is the part of the body Aries rules. You often find Aries injures the head more than any other part of the body. *Headstrong* is an Aries word and a fundamental aspect of the Aries character.

It is rare to find an Aries who hides away from life. Because they are focused so intently on their own adventure, they are out there engaging fully in life. Hotheaded, impulsive, spontaneous—the urge is to explore this fascinating world, to trailblaze.

Mars is the planet of aggression and competition, so it is not surprising to find that Aries natives tend to be natural sportsmen and women. There is an instinctive desire in the ram to pit himself or herself against others—and with all of that red-hot energy, sport is the obvious outlet. Top athletes often have Aries (and certainly Mars) prominent—and most Aries are naturally gifted physically, even if they don't choose to develop their talent to a competitive level.

The courageousness of Aries needs to be matched by a partner who is equally willing to embrace life head-on. Well, as near to that as possible. Aries' competitive instinct kicks in very readily, and so there will be challenges issued to step out as bravely as she does. Aries needs a robust relationship, with a partner who is unafraid to embrace life with some degree of gusto, enthusiasm, and impulsiveness. If this isn't part of the deal, if you are not this kind of person, you will find your Aries partner will disappear. She might be there in body, but her spirit has moved on and left you behind. Her body will follow eventually; make no mistake about that. Life won't stop to wait for you with Aries for a partner. You are either all in, or all out.

Aries' ability to move on and not hold a grudge means there is a ton of willing energy to start again. In relationship, this is a valuable gem—and one that needs to be treasured and honored. The Aries ego, when it takes a knock or three, has the capacity to pick itself up and keep moving forward. It might retreat for a while to lick its wounds, but it won't linger there. Aries has a remarkable talent for living in the present moment—and this makes for a life that has the potential, consistently, to make over, to begin again. The notion that every second is a new beginning is a very Aries concept. Each day is the beginning of the rest of your life; no one knows that better than an Aries.

Life with a fully conscious Aries partner can be incredibly vibrant, as long as you remember that willfulness is not to be overcome with more willfulness. Rather, allow your Aries partner the freedom he needs to be who he is, to be fully alive. Tie him down with emotional strings and no one will win. He needs to act on his own impulse—and when he is given the freedom to do so, he will love you like there's no tomorrow. He lives in the *now*, remember, and that's the most powerful place to be.

Love, joy, passion, and adventure can only happen in the present moment. Let resistance go, then, and allow. You are in partnership with a pioneer and this is his motivation in life. Aries will show you what an adventure life can be, if you are up to the pace.

Aries needs to feed its inner Sun through courage. The soul who has come in with an Aries Sun is learning about his or her ability to handle courage, to be scared and still function. It is not about the absence of fear; it is about feeling the fear and doing it anyway. The Aries soul has to have action . . . how can you know courage if you don't engage in life? To sit home and watch TV, or to work day after day in a repetitive, boring job is slow poison to this soul, who has come into this life to cut new trails and to bring all the experience of past incarnations together to the creation of something new. The pioneering spirit of Aries needs to be fed for this soul to feel fully engaged in life. The life force dissipates when he cannot be first. He is not a follower, but a leader. To be fully alive, vital, and energized, Aries needs to wake up in the morning and do Aries. Move, take action, embrace life head-on. Aries needs to take on new challenges regularly. Aries' solar function is at its best when she acts boldly in the world.

Aries the Dark

The dark side of Aries can be intimidating—to say the least. Be warned: Aries doesn't like being told what to do! Willfulness? Yes, to the max. Here is the person who will scream at you in an angry outburst of potent fury, cut you off with a withering one-liner, freeze you out with eyes as mean as hell. And all it took was a simple *no*. Opposition to the wishes of an Aries must always be undertaken with caution. If you've read the above, you will know by now that Aries' primary impulse is freedom. Freedom of action, thought, speech. Aries needs this freedom because he is on a journey to realize his fullest capacity to be totally alive and present. Aries shows up for life 100 percent. Heaven help you if you try to thwart the will of an Aries.

His god, remember, is Ares, the god of war. Ruled by Mars, the planet that presides over assertion, fighting, courage, and aggression, Aries is a warrior at heart. This warrior may come wrapped in the package of a sweet, smiling young man; a seductive supermodel; or the nice lady next door. But rest assured: under that warm smile lies a will of steel. Aries isn't about to give up its desires for anyone or anything.

Compromise, accommodation, cooperation, or *for the sake of peace* are not part of Aries' vocabulary. Aries will make his views known, in the most direct way imaginable. You hadn't asked for his opinion? Never mind, you'll get it anyway. And if you disagree, there is nothing Aries excels at more than arguing. You'll give up first, guaranteed. (Unless you're an Aries yourself, that is.) Aries will talk louder, employ more expletives, sound more knowledgeable, and confound you with the most intelligent-sounding arguments—all in the quest of getting his own way. His own way, of course, may be as simple as "I'm right, you're wrong." What can you do? You'll need to be in possession of a formidable armory of debating skills to outwit an Aries. You'll need to be able to think on your feet. And what's more, you'll need the energy and determination to stick in there and fight. When it comes to fighting, Aries will win hands down. Why even bother?

In many ways, for all its excitement, it can be a heartbreaking ride being in a relationship with Aries. We all need to feel that we are in relationship with the person we love. With Aries, it can so often feel as if we're not—in a relationship, that is. The word *relationship* is a Libran word, and Aries is diametrically opposed to Libra in the zodiac. That means the concept of relationship—of considering the needs of others, of compromising, accommodating, and cooperating—just do not come naturally to Aries. In some ways, knowing that will (hopefully) help. In other words, it's not about you! It's not your fault. It is, as always with Aries, all about them!

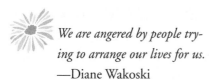

We are angered by people trying to arrange our lives for us.
—Diane Wakoski

Aries' ego is oriented toward the fulfillment of a need to be free and independent, to fight for herself and her physical survival in the world, to be fully alive and to experience all that life has to offer in order to know herself. Because this impulse is uppermost in the Aries character (and anyone with an Aries Sun has Aries energy strong in her character), those principles that are antagonistic to the fulfillment of Aries' needs, such as accommodating others, are difficult for her to access.

Dealing with their self-centeredness, then, is probably the hardest part about being in relationship with an Aries. To Aries, nothing is more important than her own impulses to do as she pleases. And that means even you must come second! It can be hard to realize, but better to know it at the outset. It doesn't mean Aries won't love you to bits—just that her needs, wants, and desires will always come first.

Arian intense self-orientation often manifests as impulsiveness. The "me first" energy is never far from the surface. It's "my way or the highway" with Aries, and he doesn't hesitate to let everyone know it. It can be difficult to live with someone who shoots his mouth off—offending everyone in earshot, creating relationship wars with friends and family—and having to stand by and watch. You'll be cringing when you see others squirm under the cruel and quick-witted spotlight of an Aries attack, or simply squirm with embarrassment when he goes on and on, as he does, about himself and his life.

You may find yourself playing the mediator more often than you'd like to. You can be left with bad feelings and soured relationships—often with the people you care about. Public relations are not Aries' strong point, and as his partner, you will be the one called on to smooth the water or else suffer in silence. Either way, it's a hard call.

One of the challenges for Aries in this life is to develop courage. As explained, courage is an inborn characteristic of Aries natives—but at a deeper level, it cannot be assumed that because this is the case, every Aries is naturally courageous. Courage is a strength and, like every strength, has to be worked at. For Aries, this means taking that instinctive courageousness and developing it to its full potential. In other words, facing the fear, feeling the fear, and doing it anyway.

If you are an Aries yourself, you will know what this means. Only you know just how fearful you can be at times. You may think you are not courageous at all. But in fact you are—or you can be. This is one of the gifts of your Sun sign, and it was given to you for a reason. You are a pioneer, a trailblazer in this life—and for that, courage has been gifted to you in abundance.

If you are in a relationship with an Aries, you may be in awe of your partner's outrageous fearlessness. But be aware: behind the actions, your Aries lover may feel much more afraid of life than he lets on. Sometimes he acts in ways that would have the world believe he is brave and fearless, but underneath it all he is a nervous wreck.

It's important to know this if you are in relationship with an Aries, because you can help your partner greatly if you do. You can help allay his fears by calming the rising panic—which you will sense, but rarely see outwardly. Panic is Aries' downfall. It can stand in the way, blocking the path of what he needs to experience and accomplish in his life. He needs to believe in himself by slaying the dragons of fear. His mission, should he choose to accept it, is to overcome all obstacles, to be the true warrior of the spirit that is his highest potential. Once he has conquered fear, he is a meteor—absolutely unstoppable. There is no limit to what he can accomplish when he has overcome fear and fully believes in his own power.

Compatibility

If you are a fire sign yourself, your life with Aries will be full and passionate—as in hot, exuberant, and fast-moving . . . two souls of fire are not here to waste life. You will keep pace with each other and challenge each other, as you live to the max together. Be aware of burning each other off at times. Watch willfulness; there are times to let go—and they are more frequent than either of you may appreciate. Neither of you has inexhaustible reserves of patience.

If you are an earth or an air sign, your Aries partner is likely to be a challenge from beginning to end. Such is the nature of a fiery relationship. But with some fire in your own nature, you can play him at his own game. The groundedness of earth can be a real asset; you have the resilience to stand up to his willfulness and the determination and strength to stay on course through all of his impulsive changes of mind and mood. Air is a match verbally, should you choose to engage. Use your intellectual prowess to know when it's time to challenge him, and when it's time to quit.

And if you are a water sign—the universe clearly has some learning for you here. Fire and water make steam. Pay attention. Don't waste this opportunity. It may not be forever, but there is much to learn from the primal fire of Aries. There are lessons around the question of self-sacrifice in relationship—for Aries as much as for you. How much giving is too much? How much self-centeredness eventually breaks the camel's back?

Relationship Clues

Allow your Aries partner the fundamental freedom of living her life the way she wants to live it. Recognize, when entering into a partnership with Aries, that the impulse to do things her own way is powerful, and any attempt on your part to thwart that impulse will result in unhappiness and, possibly, the break-up of the relationship. Try to honor your partner by standing back and allowing. This takes a strong soul. Most of us project our own needs, which are usually based on (the need for) security, onto our relationship. We want to feel secure in our relationship, to know that we are safe with the guarantee of continuance. But there is a fine line between feeling secure and imposing our own agenda on our partner. With Aries especially, we won't get away with imposing our own programs. Aries is too intent on his pioneering mission in this life to even be able to recognize your needs a lot of the time. So, in essence, you are going to have to be a strong, independent, competent, and capable person in your own right in order to enjoy an enduring relationship with an Aries. Any hint of dependency will not be tolerated. Rather, it will simply be walked right over the top of, and eventually walked out on.

A working and sustainable partnership is possible only when you, as a partner of an Aries, are able to relinquish any desire to change or control your Aries. The best arrangement would be to listen, to encourage and support, to go along with Aries' plans and missions and be enthusiastic and excited about sharing them, to be there whenever you can—but at the same time create your own life, your own interests, have your own friends. There may be lonely times with an Aries partner, so you will need to be able to fill up your own cup.

This partner is one who will encourage great soul growth for you, if you are up for the task, because of this very impulse to live life as an independent individual. Independence comes first, relationship second. In many ways, this is an excellent recipe for a whole, healthy relationship. That is, when you, the partner, are able to let go of the need to be put at the top of the pile, number one on the list. With Aries, the only one who gets to be number one is, you know by now, Aries!

Taurus

Taurus the Light

We meet the second sign of the zodiac and the first of the earth signs, a fixed earth sign, in Taurus. Fixed earth—the energy is feeling heavier and more solid, physical, and stable than the fire of Aries that went before. The soul taking on a Taurus Sun lifetime is ready for peace, peace, and more peace. The peace of the natural world. Serenity is the endpoint for Taurus.

This soul needs to feel the texture of the tangible, physical world. It wants to hold on to what it has and what it knows—to feel the stability, solidity, and grounding of the physical world. The newborn has progressed to the young child—the stage of object constancy. It needs to feel the security and stability of what it knows: what it can touch, feel, hold. Life for Taurus is a physical experience—and nothing matters quite as much as the comforts and securities of the material world, the pleasures of the senses, and the serenity of nature.

Being in love with a Taurus Sun conjures up images of snuggling together by a raging fire on a stormy night: it's cold out, but inside all is comfort, sensual delight, and safety. You have delicious things to eat and drink, and the warmth of the touch of loving bodies.

Life with Taurus can be like that—safe, comforting, secure.

All the signs compensate in some way for the sign that went before, and after the crazy, frantic, go-getting life of Aries, the soul in Taurus wants peace: peace and the safety and comfort of the familiar—and the pleasures of the best the physical world has to offer.

Taurus will work hard to bring you the finer things in life—because he wants them for himself. Taurus has a lifelong affair with pleasure—gourmet food, beautiful houses, and luxury cars (as the pocket allows). Beauty in every shape and form—a lover, a painting, a wardrobe full of designer outfits, a tasteful and beautiful home—these will feature largely in the life of the bull. Aside from pleasure, Taurus needs to feel secure in life. And that means having financial security.

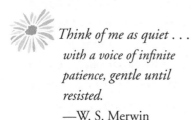

Think of me as quiet . . . with a voice of infinite patience, gentle until resisted.
—W. S. Merwin

You may have to put up with time apart because of long working hours, especially in your younger years. But it could be well worth it—because your Taurus partner is laying the foundations for a comfortably secure middle age. That is, it will be worth it if you are still around. Your Taurus lover can be so preoccupied thinking about "making himself secure" that he doesn't even contemplate the possibility you might not be around. Well, if you are happy with knowing where your relationship is going, with the certainty of "no surprises," with someone who can do the real, practical stuff of life like no other, you will be perfectly happy with your Taurus man or woman—and, yes, you may well be there, sharing the large house and all the trappings of the materialistic lifestyle and enjoying the good things for years to come.

Your Taurus lover will make you feel secure through his sheer ability to deal with life on the practical level. Most of us need to feel our relationship has a future; that it will last. Most of us would also like to know that we have a partner who will help us feel secure. The Taurus man or woman is the embodiment of security. The bull not only functions adeptly in the material world, but also has what it takes to persevere. He or she will "stick with it" come hell or high water. Whatever Taurus is doing, she is able to hang in there, take the good with the bad, the ups with the downs. Whether it's his job or his relationship, the bull doesn't quit easily. What's with this? It's about Taurus' need to feel the safety and security of familiarity, predictability, the known. The primary motivating urge of the ego is just that—safety—and peace.

Venus is the ruling planet of Taurus. Venus is well known as being the planet associated with love and beauty. Lesser known is the association of Venus (being the agent of Taurus) with the meeting of our needs for serenity, comfort, pleasure, and security. Because Taurus is ruled by Venus, this impulse is strong in people with Taurus Suns. For Taurus, the desire to be safe and comfortable and to enjoy the pleasures of earthly life are primary motivations. Related to this basic goal is the accumulation of possessions and money. Financial security is about two things: one, it provides a level of security; and two, it enables the purchase of goods and services that bring comfort and pleasure.

So now you know: your Taurus lover is going to be preoccupied with this quest, to acquire in order to feel safe. There is certainly a flip side to this, which we will look at under the shadow description. But the upside is: with a Taurus partner, you won't go without on a material level. Taurus partners, even if they are not bringing in the dollars (and most of them are), will keep you satisfied in more ways than one. Fabulous cooks, they can turn an ordinary meal into a gourmet delight—and do it on a shoestring if they have to.

Being so physically attuned, when it comes to this side of your relationship—well, it will be as good as it can be. Sex, of course, is about the dynamics between two people—but for her part in it, the Taurus woman is a voluptuous sex goddess. And the men are pretty keen, too!

Above and beyond all of that, your Taurus lover—woman or man—has the wherewithal to create an atmosphere around you of safety. But let's be realistic: not every Taurean is going to become a millionaire. A lot of them are too busy being idle for that sort of carry-on. Yet despite the fact that cash might be a bit short, your Taurus partner—if he or she is a true Taurean—will somehow, some way, make you feel safe, calm, and snug as a bug in a rug. Home will be a haven of comfort and tranquility. If your Taurus partner is not actively employed and bringing in big bucks, his calming, serene presence will be a balm to your soul. Not only that, but he will be able to create, build, make things—many of them are gifted artisans—and you will soon realize it is the journey that counts, not the destination. Your Taurus partner, every day, knows how to make your life together an oasis of comfort, pleasure, and security in the midst of the frantic world that is knocking right outside your door.

Taurus needs to feed its inner Sun through serenity. The soul with a Taurus Sun is ready for a peaceful life. To feed the fire of the spirit in him, this soul needs to attune to nature, to spend time in the natural world, to be calm, to be slow. The Taurus Sun is here to experience the physical world, to enjoy the richness and texture of it, to take pleasure in the physical senses. Taurus needs to feed his spirit, his inner Sun, by slowing down.

Peace and serenity in the outer life paradoxically energizes this soul. With serenity he can reach into his inner being and create in the world, building in form with purpose, strength, and beauty.

Taurus the Dark

The nature of life is movement, growth, change. Without this, life is static, we atrophy, bore ourselves to death, and live lives in a comfort zone that we may eventually realize has become our prison. This sad state is the lure of the dark side of Taurus. To live life in such a way—so safe, so unchanging that it becomes a prison of predictability (and, what's more, terribly, terribly boring)—can be the fate of the unenlightened Taurean. Change isn't safe in Taurus' eyes.

If you are in a relationship with such a Taurean, you may initially love the warm comfort of safety your partner provides. It can be a balm to the soul, especially if you have recently emerged from navigating troubled relationship waters. To meet up and fall in love with Taurus is like landing on solid, safe ground. Phew! It feels good. You're safe, you've come home. It feels so secure that you give thanks and vow you'll never leave. The house is cozy, the food is great—and the sex is unbelievably . . . physical!

But after a time, you may start to resent the rigidity of your Taurean lover. There is a resistance there that can feel like a very solid, very large block of concrete. If you suggest changes, even teensy weensy ones, they are

Firmness is that admirable quality in ourselves that is detestable stubbornness in others.
—Anonymous

met with silence or stubborn refusal. If you go ahead and make those changes, be prepared to suffer a torrent of unrestrained aggression, as the legendary Taurus temper erupts from the depths of that normally calm exterior—bringing to mind the metaphorical bull in a china shop. This bull you've hitched yourself to is a formidable opponent, should you be in the mood to do things differently from the way your Taurean desires. The reason the bull has awakened from its slumber is because your desire to do things differently has aroused his innate fear. He needs to feel secure.

This dark side only manifests if the natural urge of Taurus to seek and sustain a feeling of security becomes threatened. Anything new and unknown has the potential to bring up his fears.

As with all of the signs, there is a fine line between meeting the primary urge (in this case for safety and security) and having the urge implode in on itself—resulting in dysfunction. Taurus' dark side is resistance—downright stubborn, dogged, immovable resistance. It can be a hell of a thing to live with, and the only answer is for you to be as pliant and adaptable as he is stuck— because two stuck things don't go very well together. One of you must be capable of bringing in new energy and openness, or you will both drown in a sea of wet concrete—which will soon harden and eventually crack from internal pressures: those of unmet needs to change and grow, soften and flow, with life.

Hopefully, through your example, your Taurus partner will come to see that change needn't be quite as terrifying as she thought it was. You'll need to start with the small things though. Don't expect to suggest picking up and moving overseas and have it met with a resounding yes! Those sorts of changes will be entertained by an evolved Taurean only—and probably one with a hefty dose of the mutable element in her chart (Pisces, Sagittarius, Gemini—Moon or Ascendant). The obsession Taurus can have for stability at every level has other dark fingers.

Interpersonally, it can manifest as a deep intolerance of change in others. The nature of life is growth and change, and that applies to all of us—as we evolve through our life's journey. In relationship, the natural flow of evolutionary change can be seen as a huge threat to Taurus.

This sign is the second in the zodiac, and so it comes in the group of what are known as *personal signs*. As the name suggests, these signs (Aries, Taurus, Gemini, and Cancer) are predominantly oriented toward the meeting of their personal needs (as opposed to the social and universal signs that follow them). They exhibit a relatively selfish and childlike outlook in terms of their need to fulfill their own needs and desires ahead of consideration for others. Now, remember that all of us have Taurus (and Aries, Cancer, and Gemini) somewhere in our charts, so to a lesser or greater degree (depending on the planets that occupy these signs in our charts), we are all infant-like and selfish. We are talking here about Sun Taureans, which means the Taurus principles are strong characteristics of the personality. However, this is not to suggest that this group is necessarily more selfish than, say, those born with the Sun in Scorpio—simply that a primary impulse for those born with the Sun in Taurus is to meet their own needs first.

The preoccupation of Taureans with stability may be further entrenched by a resistance to allowing others to have their way. And we're talking here about change as it naturally occurs through the life cycle. Not only is an unconscious Taurus partner then likely to deeply resent and resist your personal developmental changes, but he is also likely to act out this resistance in ways that can be extremely childlike and selfish. This is the dark side of Taurus' safety and comfort: "No! You can't change! I want things to stay just as they are!" Underneath the protestations, sulking, toy throwing, and temper tantrums is, of course, fear. Fear is always the basis of the shadow.

Another dark finger belonging to the hand of the Taurean shadow is that of overextended materialism. The flip side of an inborn talent to acquire and possess, to accumulate and own, is a preoccupation with "stuff." And a preoccupation with stuff does not contribute to an unencumbered spirit. It does the opposite: it burdens one, as the weight of materialism is heavy. Everything you have wants to own *you*. There is no escaping the fact that the more we have, the more it has us. And for Taurus this can be a real dilemma. They start out thinking that the more they have, the safer they will be. More money means greater protection from the vagaries of life. First-class passengers get to the leave the aircraft first; they get better treatment, they're looked after, they can take better care of them-selves. Wealthy people can afford the best in health care—protection from the slippery and fateful hand of illness. In fact, death itself, the ultimate fear, can be kept at bay (some of these deeply materialist types believe) if you've got enough money.

In order to get to this place, Taureans can be acutely competi-tive, though not in the overt way of Aries. Taurus competitiveness is more veiled. You wouldn't know Taurus is on a mission of get-ting to the top of the heap because she doesn't brag about her suc-cesses along the way, like Aries does. Of course money can buy us a measure of security, the best things in life, and the freedom to enjoy them, but it cannot insulate us from the dark side. There will still be relationship problems, health problems, worries with the kids (children from the most affluent homes are no more pro-tected from life-pain than other kids). It can take a long time for Taurus to realize this.

The problem Taurus has is that she very often doesn't know when enough is enough.

She wants to feel safe, and ends up feeling burdened. Life becomes an endless treadmill to acquire more and more and more. The pursuit of stuff begins to crowd out the spirit.

Taurus can be guilty of confusing material possessions with actual love. Concrete manifestations of love (gifts, jewelry, flow-ers) become tangible substitutes for the real thing. It is all well and good in the mind of the Taurean doing the giving; but for the receiver, after a while, "things" can feel a tad hollow. Yes, nice bracelet, but I'd really prefer you to *tell* me that you love me, to put your arms around me and listen to me. As an aside here, if your partner has Venus in Taurus, the above will be her primary way of expressing love—i.e., through giving material things.

If Taurus can stop rushing about like a mad thing trying to make life more secure for himself, or else sit back in a state of unadulter-ated indolence, then he just might be in a position to be there for you—to relate to you with all of his ruling planet's good grace and equanimity. That is, if he is not held too far under the spell of the dark side of his sign—the bewitchment of the material side of life.

Compatibility

If you are an earth sign yourself, you will resonate with the calm and steady qualities of Taurus. An enduring relationship is likely when two earth people come together. They have what it takes to weather the storms of life.

With fire and air, the going gets a little tougher. You can complement each other well—fire breathing life into Taurus and air inspiring her with new ideas and contacts—but only if you can each honor your differences, since your natures are fundamentally quite different. If not, the flip side will be frustration—the immovability of a Taurus entrenched in the tried and true versus the overly mobile energy of fire and air, who cannot easily slow down to smell the roses.

Water and earth can make mud. On the other hand, water quenches parched earth and brings life. Earth gives water somewhere to land, something to hold on to, an anchor. These two can be very good for each other. Mud happens when water and earth manifest their dark sides together. Aim for the light sides of your Sun signs and you will stay on course.

Relationship Clues

Love your Taurean constantly. Be constant in your reassurances of your loyalty and your love, because Taurus needs desperately to feel secure with you. Many Taureans will stay with partners who treat them very badly—and this is a very sad thing. They do it because they would rather be with the devil they know. A lovely Taurean man, married to a somewhat neurotic, aggressive, and demanding woman, was heard to say: "I know she's a bitch, but she's *my* bitch." That pretty much sums up the Taurean philosophy when it comes to partnership. The thought of separating, of finding someone better is just too daunting, because it would mean letting go of the comforts and familiarities of the one he knows. Even uncomfortable comfort zones can feel good, once they have become familiar. Taurus can hang in there way past the use-by date.

If your partner is born under the sign of Taurus, please be kind. These people have warm hearts and gentle souls (most of the time); and with the planet of love as their ruler, they need to feel love. Try to de-emphasize the material side of life. Taurus needs some help here.

Help your Taurean to appreciate the simple pleasures and assure him that you don't need all the material trappings to be happy. If you collude with his inborn fear of lack on the material level, he may well become driven to acquire and accumulate money and possessions—at great cost to your relationship. Taurus is happiest when she feels serene and with a level of comfort, which needn't be excessive or opulent. She is capable of creating beauty and an atmosphere of peace and tranquility out of minimal resources. Another thing: watch the diet. Taurus has a love of good food (and drink), so he may need some encouragement in that direction to avoid putting on too much weight.

Help your calm and steady Taurus lover, your rock in a world of uncertainty, know that he is loved unconditionally, irrespective of how much or how little you own together. Help him to see it is only your love that matters, and everything else is a poor second— and that your loyalty and commitment to be there through all of life's hard bits is an absolute, unquestionable given. Your constant reassurances are balm to the soul for Taurus. And for you, your determination to honor your relationship above all else and your ability to keep the tides of change at bay—even those, or especially those, within your own soul—will be a powerful impetus for enlarging your life from the soul level. After all, it is not in the outward world that real power lies, but in the continuing commitment to consciousness and expansion of the soul. Your Taurus partner is capable of giving you more gifts, more precious soul gems, than you may yet realize.

Gemini

Gemini the Light

Now the young soul has reached a place of safety in the world, and is ready to learn about this fascinating environment it has ended up in. Leaving behind the need for security and the solidity of the earth, Gemini, the first of the air signs, is mental energy embodied.

Endless learning and a sense of wonder are the endpoints for Gemini. The soul experiencing a Gemini incarnation has a great and pressing need to acquire knowledge. His inner Sun is fed by broadening his understanding of life—opening up to new belief systems, fueling his mind with new information. Gemini is the young child, eager and curious about the world. The Gemini soul is like the child, in a constant state of restlessness. Here the soul is open to life—and this openness must be kept alive, or his soul will shrivel. Ruled by Mercury, Gemini is quick, agile, busy in mind and body. Life is short, and there is much ground to cover.

To feed his inner Sun, Gemini needs to satisfy his curiosity, to learn all he can about the world, and to embrace change.

Being in love with a Gemini Sun can be a fascinating, exhilarating, and above all, an educational experience. Your Gemini will keep you on your toes for sure, as he switches and swaps, chops and changes, in his endless pursuit of new experiences. Your Gemini lover will skim over the surface of life: up one moment, down the next. She'll laugh with you, then five minutes later snap at you. It will be exciting, but exasperating, living life with this mistress of unpredictability. Her changing fancies, while not as dampening as the brooding moodiness of Cancer, are nevertheless a challenge to keep up with. No point in trying, really.

If you love this person born under the sign of the twins, it's best to just shut up and let go. Free her to get out and about and grab life with the exuberance that only she can. If you try to rein her in, she'll probably do it anyway. She'll make friends with the most interesting people and host sparkling parties. Life will be lively and full of fun and excitement. It's only a slight exaggeration to say she'll change her hair, her style, and her job with greater frequency than most people change their underwear.

Male Geminis are just as intent on doing their own thing. This isn't the self-centered "my way or the highway" of Aries. It is more the endless fascination with learning and acquiring information that propels Gemini to keep moving. It's just unfortunate if you can't keep up, because he can't really stop to wait for you.

All the better if you are equally as intent on avoiding letting the grass grow (perhaps if you have a Gemini Moon or Ascendant). But if you're as fickle as your Gemini is, then there could be problems. Someone in this partnership needs to be a stabilizing influence.

Socially, this sign sparkles. Geminis are in their element when they are at a party. They love to chat, gossip, move from one person to another. They loathe missing out—so they're not made to sit wallflower-like and watch the action. No, they're more likely to be leading the charge. They're not slow in making approaches to people they've never met; in fact, they love to make new acquaintances. Gemini really enjoys the whole business of social intercourse. They don't mind the other kind too much either—but unless that mental rapport is happening, connections on a more physical level are less likely to be pursued.

> *It is terribly amusing how many different climates of feeling one can go through in one day.*
> —Anne Morrow Lindbergh

Being an air sign, Gemini is far more tuned in to the world of thought and ideas than the sensual. The earth signs love the body, and the fire and water signs find affinity there, too—but the air signs are the ones that can generally take it or leave it. (That is, unless they have heavy doses of Scorpio or Taurus energy in their chart.)

If you are in a relationship, the physical is very important to you. But if you find your Gemini lover is sometimes difficult to get going, the reason is: it's all to do with the mind. Oh, don't get me wrong—Gemini can be as passionate as the next person. But this sign is more likely to lose interest or disconnect due to "mind stuff"—interference from the intellect, old patterns from the past that get played out again in relationships. Gemini's desire for new experiences doesn't mean he has relinquished the hold of his history (unless he's particularly conscious). Family background is a good indicator of the patterns you can expect to see in your relationship. That is, if your Gemini man had a loving and adoring mother, he will know how to treat you. If his mother withheld affection and was emotionally distant, then he may have difficulty connecting in true intimacy. Ditto, your Gemini woman: if her relationship with her father was positive, the stars are looking brighter for your relationship.

Looking at it positively, Gemini's flair with words and ability to make connections means your relationship has many other dimensions on which to play. And reconnections can be made through the power of communication.

That means you can find levels of connection with your Gemini lover beyond those of the physical. All you women out there who want a man with whom you can actually have a conversation, check out a Gemini. If you are with one already, you'll know that if you connect on this level, everything flows. The secret is to be open enough to accommodate the restless energy of mercurial Gemini.

Mercurial is the word we give to people who are rapid-fire, quick to change their mind and their movements. This is the word that describes Gemini—whose ruler of course is Mercury. Light on their feet, quick in movement and thought, with Gemini as lover, life is rapid-fire. If you are an intellectual sort, that's good news. If you're not, you'll be amazed at what you'll learn with this Jack- or Jill-of-all-trades. They know a bit about a lot. Both sexes can fix things and make things (albeit in a rudimentary fashion), because they aren't afraid to try. They see life as a big experiment, and you learn as you go! There is a refreshing, childlike quality to Gemini that is quite captivating. These people can crack jokes and entertain; their quick repartee and their breadth of knowledge on anything from climbing mountains to making marmalade is staggering.

Breadth is the operative word. If you are looking for depth, then sorry to disappoint but Gemini is not big on it. The rare Gemini will dive deep into life's deeper waters, but most of them cruise through life on the surface. They may have many jobs, lots of interests, and lots of relationships, which brings us to an important point.

Because of the dual nature of this sign, legend has it that a Gemini usually has at least two marriages. If you happen to be the first, don't despair. As long as you can keep the interest of this restless soul, you should be happily able to maintain life in the fast lane for many a good year. And these "legends" are, after all, old energy. We are moving very deftly into a new energy on this planet, and many of the old stereotypes, in astrology as elsewhere, are rapidly becoming irrelevant. Look to the essence of the Sun sign of your partner—and through a little accommodation to it, magic can happen.

When all is said and done, what's not to love about a partner who is the life and soul of the party, who knows more about more subjects than anyone else you know and can entertain you with her sweet innocence and curiosity? The proverbial Peter Pan, this one—so if you're a bit of a Wendy (ready to fly on a whim!), this relationship could be quite an adventure.

Gemini needs to feed its inner Sun through continual learning. The soul with a Gemini Sun will starve if it isn't able to satisfy its sense of wonder. Curiosity for this soul is not something to be left behind in childhood, but something to be felt throughout the lifespan. Feeling wonder and curiosity feeds the spirit of the Gemini soul. In order to engage in life with passion and remain energized, this soul must keep learning, keep opening the mind to the mysteries and knowledge systems of the world. This sense of wonder feeds the inner Sun of Gemini. To close down the mind is death to this soul. And Gemini needs to keep moving. To get stuck in any sort of repetitive rut, job, or lifestyle atrophies Gemini's life force bit by bit.

Gemini the Dark

Now things get interesting. You thought it was all lightness and brightness, fun and frivolity (unless you are already with a Gemini, of course, in which case you know quite well that isn't the whole truth). In fact, at least half the time—when Dr. Jekyll turns into Mr. Hyde—life with Gemini can be more annoying than entertaining.

The fickleness of Gemini, while charming in its freshness of attitude, can equally create frustration. You can talk to your Gemini partner, pouring out heart and soul, only to realize that he hasn't heard a word you've said. He's been much too preoccupied with his own thought processes. It's true: when you first met, he seemed to hang on your every word—looking into your eyes, finishing your sentences for you. But that time passes; and with Gemini, those days of fascination are over all too quickly. After all, life is full of interesting new things to discover, and let's face it, he figures he's learned pretty much all there is to know about you by now (ouch!). *New*, then, can equate to people as much as to any other subject. Here is the basis of the generalization that Gemini people usually marry twice (at least!). On reflection, with second marriages more the norm now, perhaps we should increase that generalization with Geminis to at least three marriages.

It can be wounding, deeply wounding, to realize that this man or woman you love, and probably agreed to marry far too early on in your relationship, is no longer fascinated by you. It was intoxicating to have felt so heard. It was as if no one on the planet before Gemini came along had been so riveted by the things that came out of your mouth. Nothing that good could possibly last. Now when you come home at night, he seems more enthusiastic about the evening news than about the events of your day. In fact, he has probably long since given up asking you about them. You might be doing your best to "connect" by striking up conversations about this and that—the little nothings of your day. Talking was the area that once brought your relationship to life. But the Gemini partner who has lost interest mentally is really a bit of cardboard cut-out to live with.

A sense of wonder is the Gemini intent, and this is, of course, the charm of this mutable air sign. The flip side of a sense of wonder is a loss of grip on reality.

Unless your Gemini lover is anchored to the "real world" with some strong earth signs prevalent in his chart, he might be so dragonfly-like that living among mere mortals on the mate-rial plane can be beyond him. It is the fascination with the next subject, the restlessness, the highly charged nervous system that creates the impulse in Gemini to move on to the next question—usually before he has allowed himself time to consider his answers to the first one. If you try to pin this (less conscious) Gemini down, you may be in for a hard ride. Gemini is happiest on the surface of life. Commitment can be a problem with this sign, although usually it is more an issue with the other air signs, as Gemini can jump in with all that initial enthusiasm at having found a like mind before considering all other aspects. Considering consequences is not generally a Gemini strength. The impulse is to move quickly in order to cover the most ground possible. With this motivation barking at her heels, it really can be mightily difficult for Gemini to "get real" enough to cope with things like long-term careers and enduring marriages.

My dilemma . . . is to force the two poles of life together, to transcribe the dual voices in life's melody.
—Hermann Hesse

Now you see where the Gemini "multi-marriage" reputation comes from. Fickleness and stability rarely go hand in hand—and it is stability we need in order to create relationships that are capable of withstanding the vicissitudes of life as a twosome.

Gemini is one of the four signs known as *personal signs* (the other three are Aries, Taurus, and Cancer). The personal signs are characterized by their egocentricity. Now, before you feel offended, you Geminis out there, take note: we all have Gemini somewhere in our charts. If your Sun happens to be in Gemini, it means your most conscious impulse is to consider your own needs first. For those of you in a relationship with a Gemini, this simply means that these people can be babies at times! They don't instinctively consider others' needs before their own. They are usually so intent on their own mission, which is one of discovery, learning, and living with a sense of wonder (often turning to confusion because of the proliferation of information dancing around their mind-space), that they seem to be incapable of understanding your perspective.

Now, if your Gemini has a Pisces Moon or a Cancer Ascendant (for example), then you are fortunate, because she is likely to be more interested in you and your needs than she would be without the feeling, watery signs prominent. It will be part of her emotional repertoire to be compassionate, sensitive, and caring. However, even then, it will be her butterfly quest to taste the next flower that will prevail—above and beyond all else.

It isn't that Gemini means to be unkind or uninterested; it's just that the underlying drive of this sign is to learn and discover. Naturally enough, relationships require us to invest some of our energy in "the other." While Geminis are interested in you at the start, fascinated even, should they fall in love, like everything else in their lives their curiosity is all too quickly extinguished. Yes, there are many charms being in a relationship with this Peter (or Petra) Pan: life is interesting, things never stay the same for long, intelligent conversation is always in the offing, change is embraced—but the dark side has the potential to counter all that is light and bright and breezy. Geminis who have grown bored can be a work. But if you love your butterfly, you'll do what you can to keep the fascination alive—and the effort will have its own reward. Life will certainly never be boring. Stagnation is *not* Gemini's middle name.

Compatibility

The air signs perfectly complement Gemini. Life can more easily be a social and intellectual whirl—full of people, movement, change. As with all the "compatible" sign combos, the danger is that of "too much of a good thing." Too much harmony can be as much a threat to a relationship as too much dissonance. Gemini can grow easily bored, so too much predictability can stifle affection. Still, these are best of the matches as far as Gemini goes.

Fire can go very well with Gemini—as long as there are some other compatible elements in your charts. Essentially, fire energizes and fuels Gemini's drive to cover as much ground in life as possible.

Earth can be a problem. You have fluidity opposed to rigidity. Air and earth—think of tornados and hurricanes uprooting the secure structures of the land. Everything needs to be balanced. When it is, you each give to the other the gift of a whole different perspective on life—and that is the ultimate purpose of relationship: to grow through the incorporation of another's perspective.

Gemini can have a strong attraction to the water signs, usually to the detriment of both. But why do we find this attraction? Because Gemini instinctively knows water has much to teach. Water knows about emotion, feeling—those things Gemini feels vaguely out of touch with. And water is drawn to the lightness and brightness of Gemini. There is much learning in this connection, so you will both need to pay attention and stay conscious! If not, you can too easily fall into the dark side and lose each other.

Relationship Clues

Make it your primary mission in this relationship to become more of yourself. As you fill yourself up, enlarge your vision of life, and engage your soul in activities that deepen you, you will do two things: one, you will live a more meaningful life and a more satisfying life; and two, you will deflect your reliance on your partner to fill in the gaps, as you learn to fill them up yourself.

We are all on a journey to deepen, to bring together our ego consciousness and our soul's uniqueness. Too many of us expect our relationships to fill the inevitable void that is a consequence of living as spiritual beings in human form (where ego and soul have to learn to live together). If you make it your quest to meet your own needs first, even if you don't know what they are (discovering them is part of the journey!), you will free up your Gemini lover to explore the scattered regions of the world of his own mind. You will become bigger, in heart and soul—and this will mean you will have the fortitude to cope with the lack of intimacy his mental distraction creates. You will also become more interesting to your Gemini mate, as you learn and discover more and become more whole. The payback of making this, at times, lonely journey (in fact, we are all alone, whether we are in relationship or not) will be your twin's return to your side. He will discover that you are, in fact, way more interesting than all those other people he met at the party the other night. You will keep the passion in your relationship alive, because you have, first and foremost, the possession of your own heart, mind, and soul.

Gemini is fickle and unstable, but in a relationship where the partner is stable in the sense of being self-reliant, there is the potential to create a lasting union that is based not on codependent needs being met, but on the source of real strength—a deep and ongoing connection with one's own soul. It may seem a lonely road, at odds with the intention of relationship, but ultimately we are all separate and our responsibility for wholeness lies not to another, but to ourselves. We cannot look to another to complete us; we can look only within. And when we do so, we find companionship, support, intimacy, and connection with our partner that only comes from that place of wholeness. Honor your Gemini mate by giving him the freedom to learn and explore the world—and remember as you go to share the insights you gather on your own journey.

Cancer

Cancer the Light

The soul has finished with its Gemini incarnation of knowledge gathering, and in Cancer it has moved into a life of learning about deep feeling. The endpoint for the soul living through a Cancer Sun is an opening of the heart to the world of feeling. Cancer is trying on vulnerability and sensitivity in this lifetime.

We meet the first of the water signs in Cancer. Water has long been associated with emotion and feeling—and with the Moon as its ruler, the most changeable body in the heavens, the energy of Cancer is intensely sensitive and vulnerable to fluctuating mood states. Such sensitivity can bring great empathy and compassion, and this soul is acutely attuned to the pain of the human condition. Cancer craves the safety and security of belonging. The pain of feeling alone or abandoned, of not belonging, can be excruciating. Life feels harsh to this one, so the soul needs to retreat from it on a regular basis. This soul has an inner child who needs to be cared for, and if it isn't—life can feel very bleak.

Being in love with a Cancer Sun means being in love with someone who you know really needs you. The crab needs to have someone to care for and look after. Cancer is, after all, the mother of the zodiac—and nurturing you, taking care of your needs, is really an extension of her own needs. Yes, the crab wants to be nurtured and taken care of, too. That's why she does it.

If it is the cozy comfort of home you want, you couldn't have picked a better sign to set up house with than Cancer. Your Cancer lover will bring you breakfast in bed, cook you delicious meals, do your washing (including the folding and putting away), welcome you home with a drink and a smile, and genuinely look happy to see you. She is Mother reincarnated. And he, well, he is a protector extraordinaire.

It doesn't take long to discover that your Cancer lover is going to be your protector and defender; for as long as you are together, you know he will look out for you. He will probably want to keep looking out for you beyond that time—but that's a story we'll meet in the next section.

We're talking here about the light or positive side of the sign you are sharing your life with. And there is a lot about Cancer that is positive. This sign, more than any other, is innately wired to feel the world; its natives naturally empathize with how things are for you. The empathy and connection Cancer evokes is like a warm blanket on a cold night: instantly comforting and soothing. Cancer has the gift of easing your fears and smoothing your furrowed brow. He can say the right things to make you feel it will all be okay. You'll go a long way to find a better shoulder to cry on than your Cancer lover. Truly! It's amazing. Now, quick insert here, this is Cancer on a good day. You wouldn't expect such emotional rapport from one who doesn't feel, equally, such pain, would you? And naturally, there's a side of that that isn't all calm and soothing.

Cancerians, in all honesty, are not the lightest and brightest in the zodiac line-up. Ruled by the Moon as they are, they do struggle with life sometimes. But the paradox is that this very sensitivity, this ability to connect with others on an emotional level, is what makes them such beautiful people to have as friends and lovers. No one else will make you feel so heard, so understood, and so nurtured as Cancer.

The essence of good mothering is the ability to care in practical ways. It's all very well to say, "I love you" to the children—but without physical demonstrations of that love, it remains birdbath shallow. Love is what we do. And Cancer knows this to his very last molecule. The crab can be, literally, love in action. The Cancer will cook, clean, cuddle, comfort, care for—like no other. Princess Diana was a Cancer Sun—and when she was a child, she loved nothing more than to do her sisters' laundry, cook meals, and pack their bags for them when they went back to school. She was a "mother" to her little brother from the time her own mother left the family home when she was seven. She later became "mother" in a more universal sense—caring for those in need of some love and comfort.

The male crab is so innately tuned in to the needs of his family that no matter where his heart may lead him in terms of romance, he will always be there for them. His children will be his children forever—and their needs, he will place ahead of all others. He may crave an intimate connection with a woman who truly *sees* him (that is, on the inside, the heart side)—but he will remain true to the mother of his children, because she is the mother of his children. The family represents *belonging* to the Cancer man, and this is his most pressing need—to belong.

I suppose the most absolutely delicious thing in life is to feel someone needs you.
—Olive Schreiner

If you are entering a relationship with a Cancer Sun, then, you should feel great relief to know you have what it takes to create an enduring bond of your love. If you create a home together, and if you "belong" together through the blood ties of your children, your crab will never stray. I should perhaps be more honest here: he may stray—if he has had a particularly bad experience of his own mother (hard to think of another reason)—but he will return as long as there are children who need him.

Likewise the female crab. This woman is a homemaker to beat all others. Yes, she may be more than capable in the world, she may have a powerful and well-paid career—but no matter whether she is full-time or part-time at home, she will create a haven of comfort and safety for all her brood. Even without children, the Cancer woman has an ability to make her partner feel "mothered." And most Cancer women can play the sex queen pretty adeptly, too. They usually have no difficulty being sexy women and mothers at the same time. This is because of Cancer's deep attunement to the world of feeling. The Cancerian can literally feel your needs before you've spoken them. There is an intuitive side to Cancer that can be most uncanny. So, juggling motherhood with sisterhood and intimate relationships is no big deal to this sign. She can switch roles as swiftly as the Moon disappears behind a cloud.

This intuitive ability to tune in and pick up on how you are feeling, and what you need to feel better, is due to Cancer's linkage to a frequency that lies beyond the awareness of the five senses. This sign functions most purely in a different dimension from the one most of us occupy. Feelings are not on the same frequency wave as thoughts—and this is where Cancer is most profoundly at home. He may get lost when trying to convert that attunement of feelings into words; she may burst into tears in bewilderment at the depth of what she feels, but feel the crab does—and deeply. The world is apt to misread the sensitivity of Cancer, as the crab so often does himself, because the world (as we know it) is slow to recognize the reality of dimensions other than the physical one.

And is this a strength? Is it light? Yes, I believe it is. Connecting on a heart level is a precious gift we give to others. Vulnerability is real strength in masquerade. When being true to her higher self, connecting with others comes as naturally to Cancer as breathing, by virtue of her deep feeling response and her vulnerability to emotions, and this is a light we need more of in the world. Quantum physics shows we can affect the field of consciousness most powerfully through emotion. Thought is also important, but emotion is where the power lies. And this is Cancer's forte.

Through its feeling nature, Cancer can do great things in the world of form. In relationship, Cancer will read you like a book— and if it is solace you need, sympathy and caring you crave, you have come home. That warm, fuzzy feeling you get when your

Cancerian partner shows you that he cares is like the comfort of a warm and happy home wherever you are—and what a gift that is!

Cancer needs to feed its inner Sun through its feelings. This soul has come in with the intention of learning what feelings are, what opening the heart means, what vulnerability is. It is sensitive and gentle, and Cancer needs to feed this inner child by softening into life. Cancer starves her inner Sun if she fails to honor feelings, if she closes down and becomes too afraid to feel. The Cancer soul must go there, or its spirit will die. It is a hard one, and life can be harsh for one with this level of sensitivity—but the gift of vulnerability is the knowledge of oneself, of one's true strength. Strength is at its best in compassion, and this is the endpoint for the Cancer soul. Compassion comes only through opening the heart and truly feeling another's reality.

Cancer the Dark

The world can be a painful place for Cancer. Look at the symbolism of the crab for this sign. (At one time, the symbol was a turtle, a creature many Cancerians are happier relating to.) The crab can retreat into its shell, hide its vulnerability, and wait out danger in safety. Likewise, the person born with a Cancer Sun. Here is the point of the zodiac most acutely associated with sensitivity and defensiveness. Cancer is intensely subjective, because it lives in the watery realm of feeling. Ruled by the Moon, that most changeable of the planetary bodies and dictator of the tides (of the oceans and of human emotion), Cancer is more lunar than all the other signs. It can be moody because it is subjected constantly to the ebbs and flows of the emotional tides that run through its veins.

To save themselves snails shrink to shelter in their shells where they wait safe and patient until the elements are gentler.

—Isabella Gardner

Feeling and watery emotion are coupled in Cancer with a personal sign—meaning emotion is relatively undeveloped. The intensely subjective nature is part of the package of the personal signs (the others being Aries, Taurus, and Gemini), which are concerned, above all else, with their own development—and in Cancer's case, their own feeling states.

Cancer, because of his sensitivity, is the classic introvert. Social situations are not his thing. How can Cancerians be at ease when they are so susceptible to rejection? Rejection is deeply wounding; it can cripple tender feelings. Where the other signs might be able to shake off rejection with a philosophical shrug, Cancer will turn inward and feel emotionally eviscerated. Cancerians may strike out in retaliation with wounding words or worse—like the crab with its flailing pincers ready to hook into you and fired up enough by defensiveness to draw blood. Or Cancer may simply retreat into his shell—never to be seen again.

Being shy and withdrawn, then, are classic Cancerian ploys to avoid the possibility of rejection. Self-protection is a strong motive. And there is a good reason for this: sensitivity must protect itself. If the crab had no shell, just imagine. It would be pecked apart by the first seagull that flew overhead. What the crab is protecting is its own excruciatingly sensitive emotions, the dark cavern of its lunar-driven feeling states.

This deep feeling response seeks a hook—and Cancer finds it in memory. Cancer, in fact, represents memory and the past, and all forms of pattern repetition. This sign has a great need to have a past to remember. You will find Cancer natives almost invariably hold on (those words again!) to memories in the form of photographs, collections of mementos, family histories, and the like. Things pertaining to roots (family and home) are important to Cancer because she craves a sense of belonging. George W. Bush is a Cancer Sun, and he was always going on about the family of the United States—as well as his personal family. It is as if Cancer, like a little lost crab, is craving to find its nest, its roots, its hole in the sand, where it can crawl in and lie warm and comfortable, beside the people and things it feels safe with.

All this feeling stuff, this sensitivity, this empathy—it can get a bit wet-blanketish. If taken too far, it can become cloistering, clingy, and downright pathetic. Like all good things, it can turn into its opposite when taken to extremes. The insecurity Cancerian emotion induces can migrate toward an intense need to hold on to what he knows. Think of the crab and its tenacious grip. This is Cancer when feeling threatened.

In relationships, Cancer will hold on to a loved one with just such a grip. He won't let you go easily. This is different from the Taurean reluctance to move on from a person or situation that has passed its use-by date. It is much more of an emotional bonding. Cancer, when she bonds emotionally, is generally there for life.

Why, you might wonder, have I put this under the dark side—when such a hold may be just what you would love in a partner?

In a word, because it isn't mature. Cancer's clinginess comes not from an instinct to see through the tough times, not from a deep respect and love, but more from a childlike desire to cleave to what he knows. Like Linus with his blanket, Cancer needs the security and comfort of the familiar. *Familiar* is, of course, a Cancer word. Cancer needs the comfort of the known, of roots, of family. And you become family if you become his partner.

If you are fine with this, then all is well and good. The upside, as we've seen, is a dedication to protecting and defending. But if you want to be seen as a person, an individual, with your own feelings and needs, then it might not suit you to be the "blankie" for your crab: an extension of his home, his shell, his safe place. This emotional neediness of Cancer has the potential to devolve into a situation where the romance has completely disappeared. The ocean your crab swam in, in the early days of your relationship, has dried up, and you're left in this stagnant pool—where there is no excitement—only the familiarity of the known. And we know how familiarity can breed contempt. It is this contempt that forms the dark side of Cancer.

The fearfulness of the crab can manifest as a conservative approach to everything in life and as a dried-up response to the world: boring job, dull, silent marriage—in essence, a shell without a living spirit occupying it.

The challenge, then, is to keep the spirit of romance, of spontaneity and excitement, alive in your relationship. You can't assume your crab is going to do it for you—she is much too preoccupied with protecting her vulnerable feelings.

What you do know is that your crab will hang on to you and her family for dear life, so you have no fears that she will scurry away one dark night. Well, she may disappear as she retreats into her shell for a while, but long-term, no, she's far too afraid of letting go of what she knows and where she is comfortable, warm, and feels she belongs, to actually leave you.

Compatibility

If you are a water sign yourself, Cancer will be balm for your sensitive soul. You know you have a partner who will be with you for the long haul—who will, in fact, never want to let you go.

Your spirits are in essential harmony. Your only danger is that of drowning together in a pool of self-contained apathy. Your partnership may need regular doses of "others" and an active social life, or else you run the risk of merging too closely together and thereby losing the opportunity of individualization.

Earth signs fare well with Cancer, too—and bring a balance of solid, practical reliability to Cancer's overly feeling response. (Except maybe Virgo, who could clash at times with the crab due to its penchant for seeking imperfection.)

Fire and air signs have been introduced to Cancer for a specific learning experience. The going will not be easy at all times, but there is opportunity here to grow together if you make the effort to walk in each other's moccasins frequently. Don't be too harsh on this soul—Cancer feels and thinks more acutely than you, and it's easy to wound with your words and your wit. Cancer is teaching you about sensitivity. You are teaching him about going with the flow.

Relationship Clues

To keep your relationship alive with your Cancerian lover, nurture his need to feel he belongs. The idea of family is vital to Cancer, so extend your heart to his family and include him in yours. Make your own home and family a haven, a secure and comforting retreat from the world outside. Mothering is an important part of the Cancer relationship, so nurture your crab (even when he's crabby) in those ways that Mom used to: food, touch, hugs, soothing words of reassurance. Remember that your little crab has an inner child who is still very much alive and well.

You can't be babying her all the time, but when you are around, be gentle. Harsh words or emotional withdrawal do nothing but deepen the wound. Be big enough with your Cancer lover to reach out—even if you feel you are the wounded party. Keep the child you are dealing with in mind, and counter the sulks with lightness and brightness. If she is going to continue to sulk, take yourself away and fill up your own emotional cup (with some more lively company). She sometimes needs to be left alone—that is, after you've done what you can to ease her pain. Her sensitivity is her strength and it is also her weakness. Be aware.

Leo

Leo the Light

The soul has now left the watery, emotional world of painful sensitivity in Cancer and taken on a different garb, a new set of clothes for this life. In Leo, the soul has decided it's going to be seen, noticed, adored, and most of all it is going to have fun! The endpoint for this soul is *joy*. Joy comes through the whirl of social activity and, more intimately, through the expression of trust. Leo corresponds to the life phase of the teenager—the stage of life where we strike out and claim our power as individuals; we are developing our egos, discovering romantic love, enjoying the feeling of being independent social animals, and learning about trust. The soul who has come in with a Leo Sun is relishing life with all its hedonistic delights. Passion, enthusiasm, determination to enjoy life—these are tools Leos use to feel alive.

Close off, close down, stop trusting, stop going out and having fun—and the spirit of Leo fades, the inner Sun dies. Open to life with gusto, open to others, trust and forgive—these are Leo's intentions for this life.

Fire is fixed in this sign, and that means it is stable, strong, resilient—and it isn't going to stand back! The energy is powerful, passionate, "out there." A force to be reckoned with, Leo is in fact the sign that rules the Sun itself. Here the astrological Sun is in its most potent and pure expression. Symbolizing the ego, identity, validation, and consciousness, the Sun in this sign is at its zenith. All that the Sun in astrology stands for is there in abundance in those with a Leo Sun sign. As the Sun symbolizes the heart, the center of power, Leo too is associated

Do anything, but let it produce joy.
—Henry Miller

with the heart and the centralization of power. Self-consciousness is unashamedly unself-conscious is this sign of royalty.

The symbolism of the zodiacal signs is a fascinating study. Take Leo: the lion comes just after Cancer—the little crab, quick to retreat into its shell when its feelings are hurt. What does a lion do by contrast? Roars, of course! There's nothing remotely retreat-like about the lion. On the contrary, the lion wants to be seen—no, not just seen, but seen and loved.

Every sign compensates in some way for the sign that went before. Where Cancer is a water creature—emotional, sensitive, quick to put up its defenses—Leo is fire: warm, exuberant, showy, attracting attention wherever it goes, loud, unabashed, proud. When it comes to being seen in the world, Leo is everything that Cancer isn't.

Not that we're into comparing. Each sign has its own qualities, both negative and positive. And the compassion and sensitivity of Cancer is probably something Leo could do with. But Leo is just not that into emotion—he is more into the hedonistic pleasures of living. The Sun is in its natural home in Leo—and the Sun, as we saw earlier, has a lot to do with validation. Therein lies the clue. Leo's primary motivation is to be validated by the world. This is the "here's me, notice me" energy of the sign. Leo needs, more than anything, to feel and to know he is being noticed, and preferably appreciated.

She may hide this need in a sort of pseudo-humility, but don't be fooled by appearances. Underneath the played-down exterior lies an ego that lives and breathes to be acknowledged. There is a huge measure of self-importance in Leo. It is rare to come across a native of the sign who sits on the sidelines of life. No, these types are the ones who hold center stage in any gathering. Leo is the peacock, the prima donna, the belle of the ball.

Not only is Leo a limelight seeker, but the lion is also the most warm, loving, supportive partner you could possibly find. True, he loves the applause for himself—but he's equally enthusiastic about applause for you. There is no sign to beat Leo for their outwardly positive appreciation of others. (Leo Moons, too.) Your Leo lover will give you unstinting approval for all your good qualities and offer you support and positive reinforcement for your not-so-good ones. Why be down when you can be up? That's Leo's motto.

Leo is intensely social, vibrant, and so full of joie de vivre that life can feel like one big party. The lion just revels in a social life: laughing, drinking, telling jokes, having fun—with a capital F. These people are creatively talented, confident, extroverted, and lively. And warm-hearted, generous, and passionate.

Leo is also quite a social climber. What better way is there to be noticed than to be at the top of the heap?

There is a wonderful self-assuredness with Leo—and being in a relationship with such a person means this will rub off on you. When you feel low, he can lift your spirits. He's so confident, so able to stand up for himself. The lion believes in himself—and this is an incredibly fortunate attribute. You might find yourself wishing you had the same level of confident self-belief, but just being in the atmosphere of it can do wonders for you, too. And the benefits that come by way of that self-belief can make your life better and brighter as well. There will be lots of friends, lots of parties, and plenty of the good things necessary to enjoy life to the fullest.

If he's a bit down himself (not usual), it's easy to pick him up. Just suggest an outing or crack open a bottle of wine and put on some happy music, and he'll be back in no time. Even quicker if you can remind him just how wonderful he is, and tell him how much you love him.

There is a real star quality to this sign—no wonder it's the sign of royalty. There is a sense of pride, superiority, and the confidence that comes with knowing your position is secure; you are "up there," with the lesser mortals somewhere down below.

When it comes to the dating game, no one does it better than Leo. This sign was born for pleasure and romance. Courtship is a natural activity for the lion. Leo loves telling his story, loves to give and receive praise (which is such a full-on part of the budding romance stage), and loves to fall in love. So if you have just met your Leo "prospect," you can look forward to some sparkling and pleasurable moments.

Note well: Leo needs her lover to be a bit theatrical, too. If your partner was born under the sign of Leo, I'll bet you have those qualities yourself—you're attractive, dramatic, capable of grabbing attention. Somehow, in some way, you will stand out from the crowd—just as your Leo lover does.

The quest for a good time is the Leo raison d'être—her reason for being. What else are we on the planet for, but pleasure? Oh that's right—to be noticed. The pursuit of happiness and an ability to totally enjoy the moment is a beautiful strength of the lion's. Left behind is the Cancerian fear of being made vulnerable and its hankering for the past—and still to come is the pickiness of Virgo, who can't help but see how much better things could be. Leo is right here, right now—and isn't that the heart of what the spiritual literature tells us to do? *Be here now.* Life can only be lived in the present moment after all.

Sounds like a pretty good mix for romance to me. If you are a fire sign yourself, you'll no doubt get right into the spirit of fun with your lion. And if you are more watery in nature—for sure your Leo man or woman will put some heat in your belly and drag you onto the dance floor of life. Air and earth, you will succumb inevitably to the vainglorious charms of this brilliant showman (or woman)—whether you can stomach it for keeps is up to you (and your ego).

Talking of dancing, here is another of Leo's great show-off pastimes. The lion is a born performer, and loves nothing more than to demonstrate her skills on the dance floor, the stage, or even the bedroom. Whenever you see "performance"—whether it is the world's top ice skater on television, a particularly confident actor in full flight, or the loudest and most self-assured kid in your child's school production—you're looking at Leo in action. This is the essence of Leo. (If those three don't have a Leo Sun, you can bet your last dollar the Moon was in Leo or Leo was rising at the time of their birth.)

Showmanship, then, is Leo's middle name. The lion also excels in many of the creative fields. It is the urge of the natives of the sign to express themselves that lies at the heart of all of this. Being a fire sign, the energy is outward, expansive, enthusiastic, passionate. Being a fixed sign, there is stability in all that exuberance—which gives Leo the determination to achieve at the highest levels. All the better to perform so superbly. Practice makes perfect.

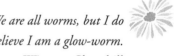

We are all worms, but I do believe I am a glow-worm.
—Winston Churchill

Your Leo lover will undoubt-edly shower you in gifts, because this sign is one of the most gener-ous. Most Leos come very naturally from the heart—a bodily system Leo rules. The generosity of spirit that prompts Leo to tell you how much you are appreciated, how fantastic you are, is the same energy that will see him putting his hand in his pocket to demonstrate that approval. It's lovely, really—and anyone who is truly loved by a Leo is a very lucky someone indeed.

Leo needs to feed its inner Sun through making life a party! The soul with a Leo Sun needs to have fun and to open himself to others, to be social. This soul is on a mission to make up for seriousness in the past, to experience the pleasures of life: romance, creativity, get-ting physical. He needs to express himself, to dazzle the world. For his inner Sun to shine, for him to feel fully alive and energized, the Leo soul needs to feel and express joy—however it comes to him.

Leo the Dark

The dark side of all this lightness and brightness is probably self-evident. It is, in a word, ego. Leo depends on attention—so when he isn't getting it, when love begins to fade, his vitality sinks. He thrives on being admired, and when romance dissolves into the accommodation stage and the thrill of it all has paled with the daily routine, Leo can feel almost panicky.

What do you need to do if this is your man or woman? Basically, work on keeping that ego fed. Even if you don't mean it (did I really say that?), try to send some praise and admiration in your lion's direction. I know it may not be totally authentic to say something you don't mean, but in this case (and there are a few) the end justifies the means. You are ultimately performing a loving action—because you now know your leonine lover needs that ego building; it's as essential as fresh air. And because she is such a drama queen, she is probably not too astute in her ability to detect sincerity. (You, too, can act.) The point is, with Leo as lover, if you want to keep the romance alive, you will need to be conscious of this very basic component of the Leo character. Appreciation, admiration, consideration—give these unstintingly and you will be well-rewarded.

There is an inherent peacock quality in the typical Leo Sun. Confident and self-assured, Leo is conscious of the impact his very presence creates. Leo is, of course, showing off. But you should understand that what looks like shameless self-promotion and vain acts that would make the other signs cringe is, to Leo, not so. To Leo, he is simply being himself—and he genuinely feels entitled to this level of attention and admiration.

Now, naturally, there are going to be occasions—probably many of them—in which this sense of entitlement creates some pretty dark feelings in associates, lovers, and companions in general. It's all very fine if you are happy standing on the sidelines, but if your own ego is in need of a little inflation, it can be hard loving and living with a Leo. So much better all around if you are the sort of person who has your own ego under control. If you don't need to be fueled up with endorsements from others, but rest contentedly in your own center (and this is something we could all do with aspiring toward), then you are well-equipped to partner up with a Leo. If reflected glory is enough for you, then this is no dark issue.

But (and there's always a but) the self-aggrandizement of Leo can often begin as a scratch and turn into a full-bloodied, weeping wound. You may be more than happy to tell him how wonderful he is in the early days, but later, as you begin to see the truth—that he isn't actually—it can be mightily hard to pretend. This is when Leo's dark side truly begins to show.

The playful cub you once romped with turns into a scowly, angry, mane-matted grown-up. He'll either sit in a corner and do the passive-aggressive thing on you (and you won't know what on earth it was that you did wrong), or he will take himself elsewhere—somewhere, anywhere that he can find an adoring public.

You'll feel bewildered. It probably won't occur to you that it was all because you didn't sing his praises when he told you how well he did at work today, how fantastically he performed. A wiser person than you would know to flatter and fawn and tell him he's the world's greatest partner and provider. Perhaps you're just too authentic for that!

Leo is capable of performing extremely well in the adult world and will unerringly gravitate to positions of power. This sign is intricately linked to the centralization of power, so these people make strikingly good managers and organizers. But, and here is shadow issue number two, because the lion is so susceptible to flattery (being her lifeblood), she can fall prey to some lowly types. Sycophants, fraudsters, sucker-uppers . . . Leo can easily be taken in by these unscrupulous characters. All the cad needs to do is feed that leonine ego. Not a few Leos have been had and lost out largely to these types.

This blindness to the faults of others can be Leo's undoing. Even Leo Moons (especially the women) can fall for the sort of person who hooks into their power (usually vulnerable and wounded types) through appealing to their good natures; and with a bit of flattery thrown in, they end up being hurt because of it. Often the ego aspect is triggered not so much through flattery and admiration, but simply because someone is giving them attention in the form of time. Call up a Leo and she takes it as a sign that you care about her, and this reinforces her sense of specialness. The Leo ego is relatively easy to tap—you can do it without even trying, simply by giving the Leo some of your time.

For the natives of the sign, however, this susceptibility to ratbags is a definite downside of a nature that craves attention. Leo Suns need to become conscious of this drive within them and learn to be more discerning in their filtration process—sifting out the fraudulent ones. For this, they can be greatly helped by having partners who acts as "truth meter police." If you are the partner of a Leo, this is something you can do to ease the pain of the dark side of your lover's ego—tell him the truth about those dishonest fans.

Use your intuition and help Leo to see that not everyone is acting for her highest good. In fact, the majority of them are not! They are simply wanting to hang on to the coattails of one who is very clearly a vibrant, generous, big-hearted, and joyous spirit. In a world of gray, frightened, and joyless people, the attraction of the Leo energy is powerful—but these trusting little spirits need protection, too.

Compatibility

Fellow fire signs, you've met your match with Leo. You'll have a ball together, so long as you understand who's king!

Air and earth—it's up to you. Sorry, but you have the facts now. In this relationship, Leo's ego is the head honcho—not yours.

And water, dear water. You have your work cut out here. If your partner is a lioness, chances are better. Lions can be too much of a challenge for female fish, crabs, and scorpions. Their tender feelings are something Leo doesn't (genuinely doesn't) understand. This relationship will be a learning experience for sure—but one the universe has surely arranged for a reason. Think about the many gifts inherent in the hard lessons, and you can create magic.

Relationship Clues

You have a responsibility in relationship with a Leo to have a good time! Doesn't sound too hard, does it? But the point really is: don't dwell too long in the negative. Leo won't have the time, or the patience, for it. You can be the best partner for your lion by keeping up the pace and getting the most out of life, and that means letting go of hurts to your own ego (it doesn't seem fair, but it is all about their egos, this relationship) and having the strength to pick yourself up. If you stay down too long, if you retreat and refuse to engage, you will wound that needy leonine ego. It's in your own best interests to keep feeding her ego. Think of it as throwing meat to the lions. Your Leo lover needs the food of your approval and applause (and the rest of the world's, preferably).

While on one level, Leo needs to learn to release his need for approval and validation, relax the hold of the ego consciousness; insofar as you, Leo's partner, are concerned, your job is not his soul growth, but rather your own. You will have many opportunities in this relationship to enlarge your soul by quieting the voice of your own ego. There is only so much room for egos in one relationship. It may be a challenge, it may feel unfair, but ultimately, this will serve you. You are not really sacrificing anything; the ego is a fraud after all. You are, rather, allowing the soul to come to the surface, and through strengthening this connection, your own ego takes its rightful place. Think of it, then, as a gift to yourself. If it helps, think of your Leo lover as you would a naïve teenager—full of fun, and full, too, of his own self-importance. Self-serving, often inconsiderate and egotistical—but all the time, craving approval and validation. A little of that approval goes a long way. And after all, the happy times make a little "ego sacrifice" well worth it, don't you think?

Virgo

Virgo the Light

The soul living through a Virgo Sun has come into this life to learn about humility. As if it is compensating for time squandered on pleasure in its Leo incarnation, the Virgo soul intends to offer itself in service to the world. This soul seeks clarity; it needs to understand its place in the scheme of things, how the parts all fit together.

Virgo has an innate feel for the details, for analysis. By analyzing, she learns how life functions. She humbly offers herself to help it function, through work and the giving of herself through her skills, her competency. The Virgo soul realizes it is part of the whole, and that others exist, that it must do its share—to contribute, to be of service. Virgo feels the desire to equip herself with skills; Virgo is the artisan, the craftsman. Here the soul enters once again the solid, practical, tangible element of the earth. The fire of passion has given way to the reliability of being grounded in the earth. A mutable sign, Virgo's earth has greater flexibility and is more movable than the other earth signs. Ruler Mercury is of the mind. The combination offers the Virgo soul a wide range of skills to choose from; he is intelligent, capable, artistic. The inner Sun of Virgo needs to immerse itself in the world of form and use these skills to serve.

The ultimate gift of Virgo is efficiency; and while that quality might not be the first thought that springs to mind when asked what you most desire in a partner, efficiency is nevertheless a positive force when it comes to keeping the wheels in a relationship well-oiled.

Here is the key to understanding Virgo: this sign represents the need to be useful, to find better ways of doing things, to be functional—all part of the quest to reach perfection. Those born under the sign of the virgin aspire to perfection through doing things in a more efficient, productive, creative way. And that perfection, by the way, is part of the symbolism of Virgo. The virgin has nothing to do with virginity in the usual sense of the word. Rather it is purity through perfection the virgin stands for. Virgo natives are meticulous, diligent, capable, competent, industrious, conscientious, painstaking, exacting, systematic . . . you get the picture.

While it might not sound terribly romantic, it is useful (a Virgo word) to keep in mind the essence of the sign—which is this desire to perfect. In relationship, Virgo will be interested in how to make things better. And you can guarantee that she will see every small, dark corner where things are not perfect.

She is so industrious that when she has nothing else to do, she sits and knits her brows.

—Anonymous

At least now you know your Virgo lover won't be content to rest on her laurels—as far as she is concerned, there is always room for improvement. As long as you are open to being "improved," this relationship can develop aspects of your being you barely knew existed!

If you are in a relationship with a Virgo, you'll know your partner likes to be useful. It is a strong motivation of the sign to be of service—and no one beats them when it comes to order and cleanliness. Often they are mercilessly fastidious. All the signs correlate to psychological pathologies or neuroses, and Virgo's is obsessive/compulsive disorder. You may see hints of this as your Virgo partner rushes around the house, gathering up objects of clutter, dusting and cleaning surfaces—like the white tornado—as if his very life depended on everything being "just so." But we are talking here about positives—so let's leave disorders aside and focus on what is great about all of this.

If you are the sort of person who likes order rather than chaos, you couldn't have picked a better partner—if you have a "higher" Virgo, that is. If your Virgo is pure Virgo, your home will be spotless, your shirts ironed, the household bills paid on time, regular and nutritious meals will grace the table, the car will be clean—and a generally efficient state of affairs will prevail. This is, I hasten to add, Virgo at its best. There is another side to the story, which we will come to.

Virgo corresponds to the life stage of the young adult entering the workforce and learning a trade or profession. Past are the carefree teenage days of Leo, when fun and pleasure ruled. Now the mission is focus on service and attaining a level of skill, in order to be a productive member of society.

If you're a bit of a health and fitness freak, you're well paired with Virgo. Virgo natives, because of their urge to function efficiently, are usually interested in the workings of the body. Diet, exercise, anatomy, physiology, and, in fact, anything and everything connected to health is innately compelling to Virgo.

Virgo can exhaust every dietary trend, rigorously work out, slavishly practice yoga, and visit every alternative therapist under the sun, as well as the conventional ones—in her quest for perfect health. Your Virgo may be unaware that the answers to what constitutes perfect health, while encompassing the physical vehicle, also go far beyond it. Don't even bother: most Virgos won't hear you on that one, unless they are "new energy" Virgos—in which case there will be an instinctive understanding of the mind/body/spirit linkage. Being an earth sign, they are at home in the world of the senses. Expect more than a passing interest in such things as massage and other body therapies.

Virgo is a mutable sign, ruled by Mercury—and this is apparent in the nervous energy these people seem to emit unconsciously. There is a restless, somewhat agitated (always more to do!) quality that comes from this innate desire to improve, to be efficient, in whatever situation Virgo finds itself. Places to go, things to do . . . the mutable element gives this earth sign a more fluid, adaptable, versatile character than the other earth signs—which are more concerned with keeping things as they are. Its ruler, as the name suggests, is mercurial in character. Mercury keeps its Virgo subjects at the upper end of the nerve scale—constantly oscillating, rarely relaxing.

There is a great reservoir of industriousness in most Virgos that leaves the other signs not only exhausted watching them but also vaguely guilty. How come they manage to fit so much in? Do they ever sleep? Insomnia can, not surprisingly, be a bit of a problem for Virgo.

Positively, such people can truly be a gift. No one makes a better mother, for instance, than a higher Virgo. These women are selfless in their service and devotion to their families. They run beautiful, clean, functional homes, and they give of themselves to an extraordinary degree. They do so because these Virgos believe they are on this planet to perform a service, to do some kind of work that will help everyone else function well. They take care of the details; they are meticulous in their attention to the small things that make everything operate more smoothly. They are not usually big-picture people (we need to look to their opposite sign, Pisces, for that), but they ensure the wheels they are responsible for oiling are well-oiled. There is often great skill technically in Virgo. Being an earth sign and one of the two signs of service, there is usually a talent for practical work—anything from mechanic to craftsperson, potter to fix-it man or woman.

If you are in a partnership with a Virgo man, you should know you'd have to go a long way to find a kinder, more considerate soul. It is this inborn urge to take responsibility and to do their best to make things perfect that gives Virgo men that instinctive awareness of your needs. They want to be of service, they want to be useful—and that means they do their best to find out what you want. Virgo men are also highly sensitive and compassionate; they really do care about others. Empathy is something the higher Virgo shares with its opposite sign, Pisces. Both signs are concerned with service, and empathy is one of the motivations behind their impulse to be of service—they can relate to others' situations, others' pain. Remember that every sign compensates in some way for the sign that went before; and in Virgo's case, it is compensating for Leo's egoism that very effectively prevents the lion from empathizing or sympathizing with others, generally speaking. (We are always speaking "generally" when describing the Sun signs. All of the above is modified according to the other planetary placements.) Virgo's path to the light side is found in humility and service—he isn't going to knock you off center stage, because his journey in this life is about something more solid, more real, than that.

> *If you're a hypochondriac, first class, you awaken each morning with the firm resolve not to worry; everything is going to turn out all wrong.*
> —Goodman Ace

Virgo needs to feed its inner Sun through offering itself in humble service to the world. This soul needs to be nourished through work. Energy comes through the feeling of having contributed, having made a difference in someone's life. Simple recognition of the need for all the details, all the small tasks to be completed, feeds Virgo's inner Sun. Clarity, energy, and vitality come in feeling part of the whole through the giving of one's particular set of skills and talents.

The Virgo soul must offer itself up in practical ways to feed the inner Sun—or it will collapse, disappearing into a shell of a human being, a body without a spirit. A life of devotion to the self, a selfish life, is the sure recipe for disaster for the Virgo Sun.

Such a life will have missed the point of this incarnation, and suffering will be the inevitable conclusion. Used well—in real, practical service to others—the Virgo inner Sun is given life, energy, and vitality flow. Life has been an achievement of the highest order.

Virgo the Dark

All that perfection-seeking has to have a downside—and it does. To see what needs improving requires one first to see what is wrong. This is Virgo's forte. To Virgo, what is wrong is all too apparent. And this isn't to suggest all Virgos are negative-thinking pessimists—not at all. But there is a strong vein in the Virgo make-up that is very difficult to please. It's forever noticing that something is lacking, something is not quite right. Virgo has a reputation for being criti- cal. These people can be difficult to please, because they so readily see the half-empty glass.

The higher types are as described before—selfless, caring souls genuinely out to make the world a better place. The less-evolved ones can turn that drive for perfection outward, making them feel constantly dissatisfied with the life they see around them.

If you are in a relationship with a Virgo, then, depending on which pole he or she gravitates toward most strongly, you may have to deal with this underlying drive—manifesting as fussy, crit- icizing, nitpicking, complaining, dissatisfied behavior.

These Virgos can be a pain to live with. Nothing is ever enough. They are constantly complaining about how much work they have to do, and by implication, how lazy you are. Quite unconsciously, these types can off-load their obsession with efficiency onto you— demanding (or asking, if they're in the right mood) you to do more! Pick up the kids, get in the washing, cook the meal (while they are busy working late, of course, or studying for their degree or going to their yoga class—their never-ending quest to improve themselves), weed the garden, mow the lawn . . . on and on it goes. Life is such a business and there is so much to do!

While we may take our hats off to Virgo for accomplish- ing so much—the flip side is we witness an inability to be in the moment, to relax, to contemplate life, to just be! And don't think you can "just be" when you're around them either. There is way too much work to be done for that.

The other Virgoan trait that hides in the shadows is a deep-seated inferiority complex. Every sign compensates in some way for the sign that went before. Leo is the sign of the superiority complex. Virgo, coming right after it, compensates by feeling inferior. Virgo's reputation as a criticizer can be just as easily turned inward: no other sign is more self-critical or self-deprecating.

While genuine humility can be a character positive, Virgo takes it to whole new levels. The dark side of humility is a self-negating, I-don't-matter-don't-worry-about-me introversion. That introversion is what lies behind Virgo's reluctance to engage socially. Compensating for Leo's brash, out-there, notice-me extroversion, Virgo tries to hide itself, modestly downplaying its strengths, continually seeing its own flaws. It's so much easier to stay home when going out means rubbing shoulders with people who seem so much better, prettier, and more intelligent than they are. The introverted ego is very much the shadow of Virgo.

It can be difficult living, or being in a relationship, with such self-deprecation. Belief creates reality; and if Virgo is too introverted, modest, and humble, too focused on its flaws, this is what life becomes—flawed. Your Virgo lover is then the one who is continually passed over at work, not invited out to play (all the invites went to Leo). She is the one who stays home with her knitting when everyone else is out partying.

The brilliant analytical quality of Virgo, which operates so effectively in the workplace, can become more troublesome in the realm of interpersonal relations. This is because heart, not head, is where we need to come from in our relationships. For darker Virgos, coming from the heart is not automatic. It is our thoughts that tell us whether we are good enough or not, the perspective we have on the world and everyone in it that dictates how we respond to the world. And Mercury rules the head (the mind, that is). Yes, Virgo can be deeply emotional—but its emotions easily turn negative, and become worry. The head is too much in the way. Virgo allows thought forms to dictate. Mercury, its ruler, governs the thought processes and the nervous system. There is an innate impulse to over-intellectualize the emotions and a nervous response to emotional stimuli.

Virgo needs to learn to discipline the thought processes. Distraction is a useful technique for them; something like going into the garden or doing some hard physical work does wonders to take them away from their worries. All the better if distractions are, at the same time, "cleaning up" or helping others.

In life, if we are centered in the mind, there are many things to worry about because the mind is the primary tool of the ego. This is the reason this sign has a high representation in the hypochondriac's club. That mental acuity of Virgo's is always to the fore—and combined with the sign's awareness of "what is wrong," Virgo easily falls into the trap of worrywart. It's not a great combination if you are looking for a peaceful life. (Pick a Taurus.) If your heart is involved with such a person, you know the score—worry and nervousness will never be far away. Some Virgos who live too much on the dark side revert to substance abuse as a means of alleviating the discomfort of all this mental agitation. But as we know, there are no shortcuts to any place worth going.

The saddest side of Virgo darkness is seen in the partner who leaves a relationship that is, for all intents and purposes, perfectly good, because of a deep restlessness and angst arising from the imperfections that Virgo perceives. To the rest of the world, the partner of Virgo is the epitome of a good spouse, but to Virgo there is just too much wrong. So off she or he goes, in an eternal quest for the perfect partner. A quest that is doomed to failure, of course. Or another scenario is the partner of the Virgo leaves first—there is only so much criticism a person can tolerate.

Eventually, Virgos may learn that the perfection they seek is never "out there" . . . it is "in here"—meaning in their own heart. Virgo's deep urge for things to be perfect in her world can only ever come from herself, from being the best that she can be—and realizing that neither she, nor anything else in life, will ever be "perfect." Nor will "perfection" come from demanding that the world change. Such is the lost cause that many Virgos end up pursuing. The sooner they realize that inner peace is about them, and them alone, the better.

Compatibility

If you are an earth sign, you have a reasonably good chance of making your relationship with Virgo a permanent and enduring thing. Then again, everything depends on your Virgo. A higher Virgo can make a relationship with any of the signs last forever—because he instinctively knows how to put the other first. And most people relate pretty well to that. However, a lower Virgo—well, he is altogether a different kettle of fish.

Air and fire signs, not generally brilliant matches, have an equal chance with Virgo. As mentioned, hook up with a higher one (and they are easy to spot; they are the ones who are selfless rather than selfish)—and your chances are much sweeter.

If you are a water sign, the same applies. Your natures have more of an affinity than fire and air do with Virgo, but all depends on the Virgo you have partnered with. More than any other sign, this factor seems to be key. As a generalization, Pisces can be quite compatible with Virgo (opposite signs often have an attraction).

Relationship Clues

If you are in a relationship with a Virgo man or woman, it would be a very good thing for you to learn techniques to diffuse the angst your partner transfers onto you. She sees the flaws and the faults—this is just her nature, but you can do much to negate these with a philosophy that refuses to buy into negativity. Remind her that perfection is in the realms of the gods, not here on earth. We are all works in progress. It is true you will do much for the relationship by being tidy and ordered, but you can't be her slave! You probably won't be as fanatical as she is, unless Virgo is strong in your own nature. It would be helpful to have a character that is able to make light of the heaviness Virgo is capable of introducing into the most mundane aspects of life. That means a sense of humor is imperative.

Your Virgo partner has a sensitive and caring soul: the higher types extremely so, the lower ones are sensitive to themselves and their needs. Assuming your Virgo is of the former group (and staying long-term with the latter would be quite a challenge!), do what you can to acknowledge this. He needs to feel that he is valued. His own ego, suffering from the balancing he is doing in compensation for Leo's superiority complex (the sign before), needs building up. It is easy for Virgo to feel left out and passed over. So he needs validating. You will do this best not by loudly praising and applauding (which you would need to do with Leo), but by calmly reassuring your Virgo partner that he is doing a wonderful job and everything is perfect as it could be.

If your Virgo gets carping and critical, it would be better for you to tell her that you are not going to put up with that criticism and that perhaps you will need to leave for a time. Virgo is not serving anyone, least of all herself, when she gives in to the lower side of her character and criticizes others. Try to establish a space of peaceful harmony and show respect for her efforts. Make her feel worthy and, most importantly, needed. It is vital for Virgo to feel that she is needed.

—————————— *Libra* ——————————

Libra the Light

The soul is done, for now, with the mundane world of practical service and the never-ending task of striving for perfection of Virgo, and wants to return to a more balanced and peaceful existence. Libra's endpoint is to achieve balance through finding the midpoint in paradox, living in the still eye at the center of a storm. Getting to this place means examining both sides, and then making a decision to act. The soul coming in with a Libran Sun needs to achieve a state of peace amid the turmoil of the world.

Libra, ruled by Venus, planet of connection, attraction, and beauty, is the point in the zodiacal circle where the soul enters fully into the adult world. It has grown up—and it is learning the arts of social intercourse. Diplomacy, relationship, communication, and an instinct for justice are its tools. Its mission is to balance the needs of the self with the needs of others, to find the compromised middle ground.

An air sign, Libra has a flair with words. In the cardinal element, it is out there, energized to push itself into the world—poised on the line between extroversion and introversion. To feed the Sun in its soul, Libra needs to feel the peace of perfect balance.

Libra is the first of the "collective signs," and this means the natives of the sign are highly socially aware. Relationship is the primary driver of Libra, so you might well think that if you've hooked up with a Libra,

> *The test of a first-rate intelligence is the ability to hold two opposed ideas in the mind at the same time, and still retain the ability to function.*
> —F. Scott Fitzgerald

then you have it made, that your Libran partner will know all this stuff and therefore your relationship will be perfect, it will all just work out.

Think again. Just because Libra is the sign of partnership doesn't mean he or she always gets it right. This relationship business is something we all have to work on, and being born under the sign most akin to relating offers no immunity from that! If anything, Libran natives seem to be afflicted by more than their share of relationship "issues"—perhaps because partnership is so vital to them that they become immersed in all sorts of relationship dramas as they try to figure it all out. The fact that they are usually so busy "pleasing everyone" (which means they can forget to take care of their nearest and dearest) could have something to do with it, too.

On the positive side, Libra is the epitome of good manners and graciousness. Ruled by Venus, Libran natives are engaging, sociable, inviting, attractive, friendly, charming, ingratiating, affectionate . . . Librans think about others: whether it is for the well-being of the others (higher Libran) or for the impact they themselves make and how they can benefit from those others (the less "evolved"). Unlike their polar opposite sign, Aries, who think predominantly of themselves first, higher Librans are constantly weighing up and trying to balance the needs and wants of others. Aries is interested in the self. Libra, the opposite sign, is interested in others.

The impulse of Libra is to act as a social lubricant, soothing and calming the waters wherever he goes. Naturally, with skills like these, these people make great mediators and diplomats. They excel at sorting out differences and getting both parties to see the other's side. This is because they so readily see the other side themselves. Hence the symbol of the scales: Libra sees one perspective, then the other. This sign is the master of paradox; its tolerance for ambiguity is unsurpassed—as is its ability to hold two different thoughts at one time. (The downside of this is a reluctance to commit, to choose one side over the other—but we will get to this.)

Social relatedness is the forte of Libra, and so life with a partner born under a Libra Sun can be one very social whirl. Attracting people and putting them at ease is something Libra does very well—so you need have no fear that your friends won't like your Libran lover. In fact, before you know it, he will be a friend of theirs as well! Libra wants to be everyone's friend, and friends are so important; there can be times when you may wonder just where you rate in the scheme of things. To Libra, everyone is important and it is necessary to be friendly, warm, inviting, and pleasant to a host of "others." So prepare to take your place as one of the gang. It doesn't mean Libra will love you any less—just that he may not be great at giving you that message! What I am saying is: if a friend is in need and you're not (right at that moment), Libra will put down tools and be there for his buddy. The fact that you had plans for the afternoon will be irrelevant. A friend in need . . . and all that. Libra loves to be needed, and his friends are an essential component of his lifeblood.

Fairness is strong motivation for Libra. Fairness and justice, and the fascination of hearing two different points of view really inspire Libra. Fairness comes out of opposition: that middle meeting place between the two polarities. It's not hard to pick the words *compromise, fairness, balance,* and *accommodation* as being Libran words.

In any situation of disagreement, should you be in a relationship with a higher Libran you will find there is always politeness, even in quite heated situations. Your Libran lover will have the manners to hear your side of the story—and this, surely, is a great attribute for any partnership. Because equal rights are important to the sign, it comes naturally to them to listen to the opposing point of view.

Yes, your Libran partner is the embodiment of good manners—and this is because one of the primary motives of the sign is serenity. Peace, peace, and more peace is what Libra really wants.

Everything these people do is in an effort to achieve harmony, peace, and serenity. There is often a lovely, calming presence in Librans—as they instinctively try to soothe any stress, alleviate any discomfort, calm anger, and generally make the other person feel better.

Being an air sign, Libra is very "mental." That is, through words and communication, serenity and peacemaking are achieved. Libran natives put people at ease first and foremost through talking. Social graces, mingling in polite society, and doing the social networking thing are their forte. Good taste, good manners, a strong awareness of etiquette and politeness seem to flow without effort from a higher Libran. These people are innately refined. So it goes without saying that you will need to be as well, if you are going to be the partner of a Libra. All the better if you are attractive and refined. Libra seeks a relationship that fulfills her desires for beauty and relatedness. The attracting principle is powerful in this sign. Yes, this can be superficial—but understanding this may be, finally, one of Libra's lessons. Probably a lesson not to be really known and experienced until the soul progresses into Scorpio, in a successive life. In the meantime, if you're in love with a Libra, this concern with appearances, harmony, and social interaction is likely to take precedence over just about everything else.

Libra needs to feed its inner Sun through pulling back from the harshness of life and finding that still center within. This soul needs to feed the inner Sun through pouring oil on the stormy seas—calming the turbulence around it by speaking gently, offering an alternative view, diffusing over emotionalism. This learning comes first and foremost through the experience of relationship. Relationship feeds the Libran Sun. The soul living through a Libran incarnation is seeking, too: the serenity of a calm and balanced existence, and this comes through finding the courage to choose. Surrounding itself with beauty feeds the spirit of the Libran soul.

Libra the Dark

Libra is, above and beyond all, the sign of the fence sitter. Equivocation, indecisiveness, wishy-washiness—this is the downside of Libra's unique ability to see both sides. It's very difficult for late September/early-to-mid-October born men and women to make a choice, thereby eliminating one option. When you can see both points of view, how on earth do you choose? Even just being asked to offer an opinion can really throw them. Libra's eternal dilemma is having to decide.

So, you might ask, what is so "dark" about this? Essentially, the tension this indecisiveness creates. Libra is very keen on achieving a state of calm, peacefulness, and harmony—so tension and stress are not well-tolerated. And yet these people have difficulty seeing that they are the creators of most, if not all, of their stress. This is the stress that comes from an inability to take a stand. Peace and harmony are difficult to achieve in the absence of self-assuredness.

I'm giving you a definite maybe.
—Samuel Goldwyn

If you live with or are involved romantically with a Libra, you will know what I am talking about. Even such a simple thing (to most of us) as choosing a meal in a restaurant can create a huge amount of tension: the fish or the chicken? Or perhaps the steak? Poor Libra. Life can be truly a dilemma of ridiculous proportions. To the less-evolved scale-holder, life is anything but straightforward. Peaceful equilibrium is the ideal—but achieving it can end up bringing about the complete opposite!

Life is essentially a balancing act. Everything we do is balanced by action and reaction. When we are in a relationship, we constantly seek balance. Usually this is done unconsciously. In Libra natives, compliancy is a key feature. There is a constant urge to keep the peace, to compromise, to speak nicely, to maintain harmony. What this can do, and often does do, is seek to be balanced—somehow.

The partner of Mr. or Ms. Compliant is unconsciously drawn in to balance all that "politeness." It may seem difficult to comprehend, but Libra can evoke, in the partner, behavior that is selfish, inconsiderate, even abusive. And no one is more surprised about this than the partner himself or herself! This is the nature of the psyche—it always seeks wholeness. Now this is not to say that harmony, politeness, and peacekeeping are not admirable qualities. They are. But they become a problem when they are promulgated at the cost of more "honest" behaviors and emotions.

The Libra personality when it slips on its dark mask looks anything but dark. It wears the face of agreeability. It smiles nicely through its interminable inner battles to make a choice. It sits on the fence graciously, naïvely you might say, but always the epitome of good manners, careful not to offend, abundantly unwilling to favor one side over the other. And it slips away from difficult situations too quickly, before anyone can pin it down or make it feel guilty for its avoidance of choosing. But life, it seems, does not always support such equivocation. With Libra's inability to choose, to take a stand, come repercussions that lie well concealed behind the façade of niceness and sincerity.

The repercussions of such indecisiveness can end up creating more disharmony and hurt than Libra generally anticipates. The Libran partner is elected to carry the opposite qualities, as we've seen, in order to maintain balance. So where Libra is saying nice things about everyone and advocating tolerance and goodwill to all—the partner of Libra can find herself sounding the opposite.

Where Libra wants to defend and "make good"—whether we're talking another person or a situation—the Libra's partner feels compelled to verbalize the other side of the story. Things can then develop into a full-blown domestic dispute. Of course Libra will try to hold on to his temper and say things like, "Well, if you are going to be like this, I don't know if I can put up with it. I just don't need this . . . " Then he'll leave the scene.

Meanwhile, you (the Libra's partner) are left enraged, feeling you've been mean and selfish and totally confused about how you came to be saying—and feeling—all of this! Somehow, what you feel will seem alien, as if it didn't come from you. That's because it didn't—really.

Another scenario is the Libran man (I'll pick on the men again) who refuses to make a commitment to his beloved. This is classic Libran fence-sitting behavior. But let me say here that Libra does have an intense need to be in relationship, so this dark face of the sign is not as common as you might suppose. In fact, commitment-phobia is probably more of an Aquarian trait. However, the dilemma of making a decision, of choosing one option over another, is blue-blooded Libran. Those types who equivocate, even in the realm of something so vital as relationships, are indeed wearing the dark mask of the sign.

If you are dealing with a Libra who cannot commit to you, read on . . . he is afraid to make a commitment because that would mean eliminating other things from his life: time with his friends, the social life he so enjoys. So he will try the classic "have his cake and eat it too." Time will go on, you'll be strung along, and nothing will change. In fact, the more you accommodate (that Libran word again) his inability to commit, the longer it will drag on, and the more demented you will become! Until you understand all of this, that is.

So then what happens? As he demonstrates his unwillingness to choose (you) through not making a commitment, you, the partner, begin to find yourself acting in ways that you'd never imagined you would. You thought you were an independent person, yet you begin to act like a limpet—pathetically clinging to him whenever you can. (By the way, reverse the sexes and the story is the same one.) The more he equivocates about wanting to be with you, the more you're determined to be with him! This is not, for obvious reasons, a good scenario. For one thing, this drive to "connect" (to compensate for his avoidance of connection) can blind you to the truth of the person you are dealing with. The more you press him for a commitment, the further he retreats from it. You begin to lose your perspective. You may sidestep the warnings in your quest to get a firm decision, one way or the other, out of him.

Libra's inability to make a firm commitment, about anything, can lead to a good deal of grief—and not just in partners. Friends, too, can be hurt by the "betrayals" of Libra's wishy-washiness. For instance, a couple divorce. The Libra Sun friend of the couple decides not to decide who to support. He fence-sits, in other words. The man is his good friend, but he enjoys social times with the wife—so what does he do? You've got it: he tries to have his cake and eat it. He manages to maintain his friendship with both parties for a while, quite a while perhaps. But eventually, truth will have its day. The universe doesn't support indecision. The time will come when one of the party wakes up to the emotional betrayal of the Libra and decides not to tolerate it any longer.

The less-evolved Libra loves to be social, and usually little will stand in the way of this. Here is the type who will choose to go to a party in the company of the ex that his best friend has been grievously and treacherously mistreated by, rather than stay in to comfort that friend. (The former is fun, the latter not so.) No other sign can do it quite as casually, or naïvely, as the unevolved Libran. Every act of choice defines who we are and what our values are. The darker Libra compromises his own integrity and undermines those he claims to care about, when he makes choices based on his desire for sociability over loyalty. It can take these socially slippery characters some time to discover the truth: they are hurting the people they claim to care about with their disloyalty that wears the face of "everyone's friend."

In perfect balance, nothing happens. We are compelled to make choices, and it is through choices that we evolve. Note to keep in mind, Libra: the most successful people in the world make decisions quickly—and keep to them. So while we need the Libran energy of mediation, diplomacy, fairness, balance, and equilibrium, we also need to know that there are times when, after consideration of both sides, we must choose one end of the pole or the other.

Compatibility

Water signs can find an attraction to Libra. Sun-sign "matches" are inevitably generalizations; everything depends on matching the charts in their totality. However, generally speaking, the water signs, despite their attraction to Libra, often wind up wistfully wondering what on earth it was that drew them there in the first place. Libra just doesn't seem to really get the essence of who you are.

If you are earth, you will have your challenges—as all relationships of air and earth do. You've been drawn together for some powerful learning, and much of it centers on finding the balance between the social side of life and the practical.

Fire with airy Libra can be a great match. Air fans the flames of fire and, likewise, fire needs air to come to life. It can be a mutually satisfying connection, with hopefully some grounding influences to up the chances of sustainability.

Fellow air signs—Gemini and Aquarius are the natural compatible matches with Libra. Too much harmony, though, can be a case of "too much of a good thing." This match can exhaust itself through an excess of mental compatibility. In other words, things can get boring. The couple needs some more challenging aspects in their synastry (mutual charts) to sustain the relationship long term.

Relationship Clues

If you are in a relationship with a Libra who leans toward the darker pole of refusing to ever make a decision, the strongest thing you can do for the partnership is to become more decisive. Sometimes, playing Mr. Nice Guy is a hard row to hoe, and you can take a huge weight off Libra's shoulders by being the decision maker. Remember: for your diplomatic Libran, choosing can be agony. As much as possible, he will avoid it altogether. Of course there are many decisions only he can make. But where your relationship is concerned, learn to take a firmer stand. If you equivocate, as he does, you'll wind up going backwards. It will also help your partnership to discuss what choices each of you will be responsible for. If you do this ahead of time, you will avoid nasty scenes and the (unconscious) impulse to balance your partner's indecisiveness and overaccommodating behavior.

In a relationship where you are seeking a commitment, find the strength to walk away. It may only be a matter of time before this gentle-hearted soul realizes what he stands to lose and understands the importance of making a firm commitment. But you will need to be the strong one here. As long as you accommodate his indecisiveness, for that long it may continue. Know that being in a relationship is in his lifeblood; he needs you more than you may think. Having the courage to break away until he makes a firm commitment will help him see that life is colorless and empty in the absence of a relationship.

Scorpio

Scorpio the Light

The soul coming into the Scorpio incarnation is learning to live with intensity. This is the soul that needs to go deep. Penetrating, honest truth feeds the soul of the Scorpio Sun. This one cannot live life on the surface. He is here to feel life in all its intensity and know he can survive it. He came in wounded, but he will go out healed.

Scorpio is the sign associated with all things taboo and dangerous—ruled as it is by Pluto, god of the underworld. Scorpio is the place where the soul cares not for the games of society, social graces, diplomacy, fairness, niceness, and cocktail-party superficiality. This sign is concerned only with plumbing the depths. Intimate truth, raw and vulnerable, is Scorpio's domain. Healing, transforming, merging—through sex or deep psychological encounter—is the quest. Scorpio is the shaman, the wise woman, the wounded healer—charged, in this lifetime, with bringing the depths of the unconscious up to the light of the conscious.

It seems so much more logical to go straight to the dark with Scorpio. Love in the world of Scorpio is never a light affair. How could a sign named after a scorpion be void of pain? The stinging, life-threatening nature of its namesake is a clue to the association of this sign with wounding. Love, as most of us know, presents us with an ocean of potential to wound. But where there is wounding, there is also, not too far away, healing. And healing is a true Scorpionic affair. Scorpio knows, more than most, the real nature, the deeper nature, of relationship, because she knows that relationships are largely about healing (albeit such knowing may be quite unconscious).

I know the bottom . . . I know it with my great tap root. It is what you fear. I do not fear it: I have been there.
—Sylvia Plath

The Scorpio native is bound up with the whole idea of merging. What is a love relationship but a quest to merge with another? Scorpio innately craves union in order to be transformed, to be made "whole," to be integrated. So for the Scorpio man or woman, love, relationships, and sex are vital. Where Libra craves a form of union, a partnership, in order to fulfill its urge to "relate," Scorpio craves the deep, soul-searing, profound psychological experience that is true intimacy to fulfill its urge to merge, to transform, to be made whole—and, thus, to heal.

Remember that each sign compensates in some way for the sign that went before. Libra can be glib and superficial in its unending quest to be the nice guy or girl. Scorpio then comes along and sweeps away the nonsense of cocktail-circuit small talk, and goes straight for the jugular. Where Libra wants to be liked, Scorpio wants to be truthful—and usually never the two shall meet. It's hard to be penetratingly honest and smile sweetly at the same time. Libra is about the mouth, Scorpio the eyes. Libra is an air sign, loves to talk; Scorpio is water and a fixed sign. Think "still waters run deep": that's Scorpio.

Scorpio's great strength, its light, is its unflinching honesty and desire to get to the bare bones of the matter, any matter. This fascination with all things hidden creates an aura of magnetic attraction that surrounds Scorpio natives. Their eyes have a penetrating gaze. Windows to the soul, the eyes are a clue to the depth and intensity of the Scorpio psyche. There are deep, dark places in the soul that need to be recovered and brought up to the light of day—and Scorpio eyes hint at the power in those depths.

If you are unafraid of the brutal honesty that such journeying entails, and you thrill at the thought of going deep, into the inner reaches of the psyche, then your Scorpio lover is perfect for you. But if all that sounds a bit dark and heavy, well, it may be better to find yourself a nice, light Gemini. One way or another, your Scorpio partner will attract to himself—or be attracted to—the dark, the taboo, the hidden side of life. It is a lifelong quest he is on to dig out the treasure that lies covered in the excrement. The Scorpio who is less successful in the quest can end up mired in the excrement himself—as seen in those drawn to the underworld, living out the dark in some form or another. But the others, the more evolved, use their penetrating skills to firstly heal themselves and then others. These people are gifted healers because of their instinct for the truth and their courage in getting down to it.

This is the potential of the higher Scorpio, though the path is not easy. It is strewn with dark and dangerous obstacles, and the victims—and avengers—of the scorpion's deathly sting. But the ultimate prize is a personal power and inner tranquility that comes from really knowing life in all its ugliness, as well as its beauty, from the inside out.

This Scorpio, the one who has done some healing work, the one who is conscious, is a very powerful individual. The light side of the dark seeker is a Scorpio native who has transcended the negative elements of the shadow and emerged, more integrated and conscious than just about anyone else you'll ever meet. There is an aura of power and magnetism, a charisma, around such Scorpios. They wield huge personal power, which may manifest as great financial wealth, or the ability to heal or otherwise influence others in some intensely transformative way.

In relationships, these Scorpios are compassionate and supportive in a benign but powerful way. It is a compassion born of a deep, soul-searing awareness of the tragedy and pain of life. And it's a pain Scorpio knows well—even if it is through having felt it vicariously.

If your lover is one of these Scorpios, you will be heard, you will be felt or perceived by your partner on a level that transcends the world of the five senses. It will be a psychic link that connects you and will have the protection of the power of the universe itself.

If you are in love with Scorpio, life will become an intense affair—passion, jealousy, eroticism . . . such intensity of feeling can so easily fall into the dark side, so you will need your wits about you.

Scorpio is not to be trifled with. If he has your heart, then be prepared to go deep with him. The gifts of one who truly knows and feels life at its roots, the source of all power, are profound ones. This relationship, this affair, will shake you, as you've never been shaken before. But it will take you deeper, higher, and further than you could have imagined—because you are in partnership with "one who knows." Scorpio knows life is lived on the visible level, but born on the invisible. We experience the manifest world, but it is the un-manifest that holds the patterns and the power. The iceberg is a perfect metaphor for life—most of it is invisible. With Scorpio as your partner, you have linked up with someone who instinctively knows the invisible. And the higher ones have the ability to use this understanding, this innate knowing, and translate it to power and strength in the visible, physical world. With a truly conscious Scorpio, life is an adventure into the unseen, the source of all power—a journey of the utmost depth, wisdom, and power.

Scorpio needs to feed its inner Sun through living intensely. Passion, truth, and naked vulnerability that come with intensity feed the spirit of the Scorpio Sun. This soul needs to come face to face with the deep, unacknowledged, hidden processes of life and bring them to consciousness. Without this depth, the inner Sun slowly dies of thirst; the spirit no longer animates the body. The Scorpio soul must create a life where it frequently visits the dark side—the taboo, hidden, psychological side—and through exposing and understanding it, transforms itself and others. The world of the invisible feeds Scorpio's inner Sun and gives the personality life.

Scorpio the Dark

Freud was only interested in the "basement of the human being," he said. By "basement," he meant the shadow, the suppressed and repressed contents of the mind. Whatever is deemed too frightening to be owned by the conscious becomes relegated to the unconscious (the shadow). Scorpio-rising Freud had a fascination with the basement notion of the "death instinct"—and a preoccupation with sex, often an area of life that falls into the shadow.

At heart, most Scorpios have an understanding of the death instinct, that impulse toward self-destruction. The darker side of Scorpio is an unhealthy fascination with that impulse. A lighter manifestation of this Scorpio fascination would be a desire to integrate whatever it is that is feared, or whatever has power over one—and in doing so, become transformed, or born into a new identity. Fear is about feeling a sense of powerlessness, and it is this feeling Scorpio is compelled to assuage.

Those who fall into the darker side of Scorpio are more interested in death and destruction than death and transformation. Both are the domain of this sign, and as we've seen above, the more conscious Scorpio will unearth a positive understanding

> *I am interested only in the basement of the human being.*
> —Sigmund Freud

of these processes. But the darker side of this sign will not—and in these individuals, the dark can become really dark. (Charles Manson is an embodiment of the dark Scorpio.)

There is in these Scorpios a natural control or repression that is born of a perceived fear of being the subject of someone or something else's control. Scorpio is linked to the concept of power—personal and/or collective power.

The ruler of Scorpio is Pluto. Pluto in astrology is symbolic of power and of all things hidden, taboo, dangerous, fearful. It is the power of a cataclysmic event, a natural disaster, or the annihilation of one's home or life situation—through a harrowing betrayal and divorce, or through death. Pluto is symbolic of power because it is synonymous with the unknown, the hidden—and it is the unknown that holds the power (through fear) in this universe of polarity.

Death is the ultimate fear because it is the ultimate unknown. Death is the ego's number one enemy—because the ego knows when death comes, its "life" will be over, which indeed it will.

With the god of destruction and annihilation as their ruler, Scorpios seem to come closer, throughout their lives, to such "events" than the average person. Somehow that part of a person touched by Scorpio's energy—in this case the Sun, or the conscious egoic self, will entertain or be entertained by the dark side of life.

How this manifests in your partner or lover will fall into a range of possibilities. If you are dealing with a less conscious Scorpio, there may be events of a violent nature, or there may be deep, dark, and shameful secrets—something taboo such as rape or incest, or a skeleton in the family closet; possibly it is one he has skinned himself.

There may be associations with "underworld" or subculture figures such as criminals, drug dealers, prostitutes, and so on. This is not to suggest that your Scorpio partner will be any of these things; rather, that this world will somehow touch her, perhaps through a family member or a childhood experience—or through becoming a victim, at some point in life. Or she may have been deeply wounded by a personal betrayal.

You will find there is, around your Scorpio lover, an aura of impenetrability. This comes from the fear that Pluto generates. The unknown is frightening, for no other reason than that it is unknown. It is this, and the fear of being controlled, overpowered, and invaded by another person or force, that creates this barrier around Scorpio people. No one is more distrustful than a dark Scorpio; no one is more guarded and suspicious. There is a natural defensiveness, a sort of all-pervading don't-come-too-close feeling about them. This is not the "retreat into my shell" defensiveness of Cancer, the scared Moon-child trying to hide from pain. No, Scorpio's defensiveness is more of a mobilized vigilance. These people are the ultimate secret keepers, because they know that secrets are the basis of power.

Don't, then, expect your Scorpio lover to reveal all. The higher types may, because they have learned the beauty of, and the need for, trust, but most of them will be like their symbol—the scorpion—ever on the alert, quick to shield themselves from danger, tail poised and ready to strike. Secrets of all descriptions will be held close by your Scorpio. You're wondering about his financial situation? Forget it! He'd rather die a slow, painful death than tell you anything about that. Probe into his dysfunctional family background, and you're liable to get stung, quickly and painfully.

No, with these people, you need to bide your time and build up that trust before you can even think about penetrating their inner space. And even then, there are some things that you will never know. The irony is that no other sign is more adept at pulling the secrets out of you! With their instinct for honesty and their penchant to go deep, before you realize it your Scorpio will have the full litany of the pains of your past, the fantasies of your present, and your hopes for the future. No one said this sign was simple.

Compatibility

If you are a water sign yourself, you will have an innate connection that could be described as psychic. Your bond may well be strong enough to take the assaults on your ego that Scorpio's truth seeking will inevitably inflict. It may be, if you are a water sign, that your bond is strong because it is forged in the well of the deeply erotic. Your relationship will have passion and intensity, desire, compulsiveness—it will be engulfing, consuming, and devouring. (You have been warned.)

If you are earth, Scorpio's intensely emotional ways will be the quench your dust-dry thirst needs, from too much living in the "real" world. You will have the groundedness to withstand your lover's forays into the underworld and the stability and sense of realism to cope with the secretive ways of the Scorpion.

And if you are fire or air—well, the universe clearly has some learning here for you. Pay attention. Being partnered with a Scorpio—light or dark (and inevitably a mix of both) is to partner with the life force itself. You will not sleep through this relationship. You are likely to experience moments of intense emotion—fuming jealousy, murderous rage, the "forbidden" thrusting into the consciousness in the form of illicit sexual desires and destructive impulses. Is that enough already?

And if I have painted too dark a picture—here is another angle. This lover of yours is going to take you into the furthest recesses of your own soul. He will show you what you need to see so that you can heal what needs to be healed. Integration, healing, wholeness—if you do this right—are your rewards. It will be very important for you to be as conscious in this relationship as possible. Scorpio is innately wounded—and it comes from somewhere beyond this life. You will need to be conscious to negotiate your way through this, at times treacherous, path. To understand what is his pain, and what is your pain, will require you to be very clear.

It may be all too easy to fall into bed with this one, to indulge the senses, to experience the depths of a sexual encounter that can take you into the stratosphere (or down to the center of the earth), but you must remain aware of the true meaning of your dalliances with the invisible side. The truth of every encounter with Scorpio is the truth of who and what you are. Scorpio is the divine alchemist—capable of restoring unity to your soul. To partner with such an "agent of transformation" is to live with your healer. Ultimately, the potential is there to recover from the wounds life has inflicted and emerge, like the butterfly from the chrysalis (metamorphosis is the archetypal Pluto/Scorpio process), transformed and ready to fly. This is the true intent, the evolutionary necessity, of your attraction to a Scorpio lover.

Relationship Clues

Being in a relationship with Scorpio is no light affair. Intensity seems to find its way into every crevice of your life. The secret to negotiating this relationship is to know when intensity is welcome and when it is not. Your intimate life is the obvious arena for intensity, and this is where wounds are most profoundly activated and, all going well, healed. Sex is actually a metaphor for transformation—hence, Scorpio's well-established reputation for involvement in this aspect of life. Great healing can take place if you are courageous enough to remain vulnerable but at the same time aware of your own need for boundaries. Your Scorpio partner is instinctively seeking healing through a sexual relationship. To be aware of this, to honor it by treating it with respect, treating it as the sacred ritual it is intended to be—this is how you will best serve your Scorpio.

In other areas of life, you would be wise to seek to lighten up the atmosphere by refusing to get too profoundly muddy. That is, if your partner is verbally annihilating someone—don't collude with it. Try to distract her and help steer her back to the middle path. She needs, at such times, the voice of balance; otherwise her nature can cause her to dive down too far. There are times when we need brutal honesty, but there are also times when we need to let it go, release the intensity of negative feelings, and come back to the surface. Understanding that your Scorpio is driven by a desire to get to the truth—in the quest of healing her own wounds—will hopefully help shield you from the hurt that such vulnerability arouses. You will be called to be honest here, in this relationship— and you are being offered an important soul gift. Knowing how to channel this, how to make it work for you, is no small task, but it is one with great rewards. Discouraging your Scorpio lover from falling down into the dark side, and helping to comfort and heal him when he does, is the most powerful gift you can bring to your relationship. His journey is one of life and death—and in facing death (any ending is a death), you will both discover the meaning of life.

—— *Sagittarius* ——

Sagittarius the Light

The soul taking on a life with a Sagittarius Sun is fired up and ready to awaken its consciousness to meaning. This is the endpoint for Sagittarius. All the depth and intensity it experienced in Scorpio has been absorbed, and now the time is ripe for a life of lightness and adventure!

Sagittarius is mutable fire—a breath of fresh air after all that darkness and intensity of fixed-water Scorpio. Sagittarius takes the wisdom gleaned from the Scorpio phase and, like its glyph of the upward arrow, fires it out—symbolizing the urge to

Form wants to tie me and to narrow down, but I want to expand my being in all the horizons.
—Ernst Stadler

expand its horizons and project meaning into what was previously submerged in the unconscious. The Sagittarius soul is intent on discovering that life means something, and it is energized to travel far and wide to do so.

Sagittarius is enthusiastic, optimistic, outgoing, and extroverted. It has the passion and warmth of the other fire signs, Aries and Leo, but with the heart of a gypsy and the soul of a philosopher. This soul knows, came in knowing, the natural laws of justice and of truth. It is time to channel that understanding into the formation of its own belief system, a personal philosophy born of many journeys and adventures in the world.

With its ruler the benevolent "lucky" planet Jupiter, the soul in the Sagittarius Sun lifetime is the soul pre-primed to experience the good life.

If your lover was born under the sign of the centaur, you'll be lucky, too, because good fortune will be a frequent visitor to your door, if for no other reason than that the optimistic expectation of good that Sagittarius holds will naturally create it: energy follows thought.

Jupiter is known as the great benefactor of the planetary line-up; that is, it brings rewards, opportunities, generally nice things into the lives of those whose energy it touches (either by way of their natal chart or transits and progressions). How much kinder that sounds than Scorpio's ruler—the god of the underworld, Pluto. But the soul born under the vibrations of Sagittarius has done its time in Scorpio and moved into the next realm of being. This life is intended to be a very different journey.

Life with your Sagittarius lover will be exciting—because Sagittarius loves and lives life to the full. Travel, because it is laden with new experiences, is likely to be frequent; new and interesting people will cross your path, and opportunities will be seized in an instant—because not to do so would be a waste of the gift the universe is clearly laying at your feet. If an opportunity knocks, grab it! That's the philosophy of the higher Sagittarius.

Sagittarius natives have an above-average craving for freedom, and this is because they want to explore the world—outer and inner—in order to understand the meaning of life. The desire for truth and justice are primary motives; hence, Sagittarius rules over higher education, philosophy, and the law. Sagittarius needs freedom of movement, expression, and thought in order to understand and then to pass on, or teach, what it has learned. Life for Sagittarius is, above all, an adventure. So if you're with him, you'd better be ready to grab your coat and fly out the door—life won't wait and neither will he.

This is important to understand if you are in a relationship with a son or daughter of the centaur, because freedom is, in many ways, the antithesis of partnership. It goes against the concept of "security"—one of the footholds of a lasting relationship. In relationship we are often compelled to restrain our personal freedom for the good of the partnership—life, when we are a twosome, is not always the carefree affair it once was. For Sagittarius, this can be something of a bitter pill. These individuals hate to be tied down. They need to be completely immersed in the experience of life—and so any infringement on this need is generally not taken well. Sagittarius natives like to know the door is always open, so they can fly at a moment's notice. Relationships can feel like a cage to Sagittarius at times, with the door very firmly shut.

Here is the interesting paradox: Sagittarius wants to understand the meaning of life, and the spiritual literature seems to agree that the meaning of life is something to do with love; so the centaur knows that the journey into the heart is one she must make. And yet the road of enduring relationship inevitably requires a personal sacrifice, the nature of which seems to go against the grain of the Sagittarian freedom impulse. Some Sagittarians make the journey to the heart frequently—moving on to a new adventure when they feel they have learned all they possibly can from an existing one. The quest for new experience and meaning is one that never sleeps, and always there is an eye to the future.

So you have been warned if you are the partner of the son or daughter of the centaur: keep up with the play, stay interested and interesting, keep learning, too—because your Sagittarius is not one for the sameness of dull routine. Sagittarius is a fire sign and a mutable fire sign at that—meaning constant movement, laced with passion. Exuberance and enthusiasm are uppermost.

There is a very forward-facing quality to most Sagittarians; they are interested in the future, and generally they have a very positive, hopeful attitude about it. Sagittarians make good consultants, advisors, teachers, and lecturers because of this optimistic and future-oriented instinct.

Life will never be dull with Sagittarius as your lover. Sagittarius is not unlike Gemini in this respect. All the signs work in binary oppositional pairs, and Gemini is the opposite sign to Sagittarius. But where Gemini is interested in learning for the sake of learning, Sagittarius wants to take that learning and extract meaningful insights from it.

Life is an adventure just waiting to happen for the higher Sagittarian, and that adventure has to be meaningful. To make something meaningful, of course, we have to make a connection between the outer experience and the inner one. This is something Sagittarius spends a lot of time doing. There is an expansive, enthusiastic pursuit of every experience he can get his hands on, and not just for the experience—but for the learning contained therein. And if you are his partner, be prepared to wave goodbye on a frequent basis if you are not as keen on new experiences as he is.

The higher, lighter Sagittarius epitomizes qualities of the farsighted, philosophical, prophetic, high-minded intellectual. There is another side—which we will come to, but the more positive characteristics of this sign truly uplift the lives of everyone around. Somehow, they always manage to look on the bright side. Their unending faith in things working out goes a long way to lift spirits and make others feel better. Sometimes the centaur is guilty of being too Pollyanna-ish, but wouldn't you rather have that than a doom-and-gloom-sayer?

Your Sagittarius lover will pursue his passions with gusto, and equally, he'll enthuse about yours. If you want to spend money on courses, he'll be only too happy for you to do so. Likewise with travel. To the Sagittarian, money spent on travel is money well spent. How can you expand your horizons if you stay home all the time?

Silly question, actually, because if anyone can do that, Sagittarius can. Inward journeys are as much the joy of this sign as outward ones. Learning is an ongoing, lifelong process for the centaur: if not formally through advanced study, then by studying alone—perhaps through an online course of some description or simply by reading widely on the particular subject of interest for the moment. Sagittarius is broad-minded, and with that comes an ability to synthesize information. A strong ethical and moral stance is concomitant with their innate awareness of "truth and justice."

Oprah Winfrey has a Sagittarian Moon—and she's made billions out of her televised social conscience. There is a strong sense of what is right, just, and moral in Sagittarius—and an ability to persuade others to see things that way.

There is a wonderful generosity about Sagittarius. You will know this already if your partner or someone you love was born under the sign of the centaur. An expansiveness of heart means Sagittarius willingly shares her worldly goods with others. To be fair, this may be tempered by an afflicted Capricorn Moon or some such thing—resulting in a fearfulness regarding material security—but for the most part the natives of the sign are known for their generosity; they have benevolent and charitable natures. Many philanthropists are born under the sign of Sagittarius, as they have a highly developed public spirit. Sagittarius is the first of what is known as the universal, or transpersonal, signs—meaning they are innately aware of the needs of the larger collective, beyond the personal.

If it's life in the fast lane and open-hearted, open-minded adventure you crave—you've struck the winning numbers with a Sagittarian. Best to keep in mind, constantly, the urge for freedom that dances through every molecule of the Sagittarian body and soul—or you could be a tad disappointed. If you are big enough to be as big as your partner is and "allow" freedom to weave through your relationship, you'll be rewarded with all of the above. If you resist the claims of your lover's soul to follow that inner directive to explore—mmm, well, you could be in for a tricky journey, because not for long will the Sagittarian heart be tied down. Good luck!

Sagittarius needs to feed its inner Sun through opening its consciousness to the meaning of life. The spirit is vitalized when the soul travels—in the outer world and the interior—the world of the mind and the heart. This soul needs to expand its knowledge and experiment with different beliefs. It needs to bring faith to its journey, to fuel the adventures of the mind with openness and curiosity, and ultimately to create its own philosophical platform, its own take on life. This journeying is food for the soul with the Sagittarius Sun and keeps the life force flowing. Life is very much a spiritual quest for the true Sagittarian, and this is how the sign is kept at optimum functioning.

Sagittarius the Dark

Finding a dark side to all this light, "up" energy is not straightforward. For most of us, enthusiasm, expansion, optimism, good cheer, and generosity are characteristics that epitomize the positive—or where we'd all like to be. But remember, all the qualities of all the signs, when taken too far in either direction, slip into their opposite. Sagittarian positives are no exception.

To put meaning in one's life may end in madness, but life without meaning is the torture of restlessness and vague desire.
—Edgar Lee Masters

In the quest to experience life and extract meaning from it, Sagittarius can be guilty of "not caring." I alluded to this in the light side—the urge for freedom running counter to the needs of relationship security. Sagittarius can too easily sacrifice true intimacy on the altar of freedom. The imperative to explore, to travel, to expand horizons doesn't always mix too well with the needs of a relationship.

Sagittarius may avoid the ties that bind, because the lure of the quest is too strong. Those centaurs balanced enough to realize that the heart journey is probably the biggest and most important quest they'll ever make will nevertheless have to be constantly on the alert to the temptation to disappear when the restrictions come on. It must be said here that many of those controls and restrictions are magnified in their own minds—something fear always manages to do.

Scorpio, you'll remember, has at its heart, a desire to go deep, to get down to the bare bones. Sagittarius, coming right after Scorpio, is compensating for all this depth and intensity—and it does so by trying to cover as much ground as possible. Sagittarius is about breadth rather than depth. And while breadth can be a great thing, bringing as it does a great diversity of experience, your average Sagittarian could take some lessons from Scorpio—lessons he seems to have forgotten in the desire to expunge the past. Sometimes in life, we are better to go deep. Commitment requires us to go deep: to focus, to honor. Those qualities don't sit too well with the Sagittarian drive to experience, and therein lies the potential for downfall of the dark Sagittarian.

Infidelity is a possibility, as the centaur sets off on his or her endless journeying. The ways of the heart so often require us to tame our wild impulses to please ourselves. There are rewards in doing so, but for the Sagittarian who is so intent on the path of freedom, these rewards seem outweighed by those that come with wanderlust and the new experiences they promise.

Life with a darker—that is, more self-centered—Sagittarian can therefore be a lot less than the optimistic picture I painted in the first section. It can, rather, become very lonely and at times grim.

The partner who does best with such a Sagittarius will create her own diversions away from the relationship, developing an independence that is itself an attraction to Sagittarius. Really, this is the only way to stay in a relationship with this type of Sagittarius. It seems we don't often in this life get to take the good without some of the not-so-good thrown in. For all his positivity and optimism, the freedom-loving ways of your Sagittarius can break your heart at times. Remember not to lean—pull away, just as he does. That is the only way the relationship will come back into some sort of balance. In other words: allow. Allow freedom, even if it feels hard.

In allowing rather than resisting, you will open up the way for your Sagittarian lover to come back—and because he has a powerful awareness of truth, the truth of your connection (if it has truth) will ultimately win over. But then again, nothing in this world is a given; if you are fated to part, you will eventually meet a fork in the road you are traveling together.

Another downside to the Sagittarian drive for experience and expansion is the very real possibility of biting off more than they can chew. If you are in love with a Sagittarius, you probably know this one well. They'll agree to do anything, with anyone, at any time. That optimistic nature of theirs just won't entertain a *no*—the quest for expansion becomes overexpansion very easily.

Overconfidence and wild extravagance are distinct possibilities. Another is a tendency to hypocrisy. Because the Sagittarian nature is so idealistic, much that comes out of their mouths is so positive, so persuasive, so optimistic and promising that others just cannot help but believe it! We all want to believe what sounds so good—and the Sagittarian delivering the message has a way of sounding so knowing, so believable. Being downright preachy is a real Sagittarian trait.

The chickens come home to roost when the Sagittarius fails to live up to the promises and ideals he has so convincingly expounded. Others may come to ruin, financially or otherwise, through that Sagittarian over-the-top optimism and faith in positive outcomes. Sadly, life doesn't always work that way—and all the faith in the world sometimes just isn't enough.

Or, in his own life he may act in completely contrary ways to the oratory. Oh yes, he believes in truth and honesty, in fidelity and faithfulness, but in reality he has a hard time actually living up to all that idealism. Partners may eventually walk away, their own faith damaged by the faithless one, who promised so much.

Delusions of grandeur can be another possible pathology linked with this sign. Generosity and philanthropy can turn into an exaggerated sense of self-importance.

The light Sagittarius wants to give purely for the sake of giving. It feels natural and good, and comes from a heart that knows the connection of one human with all humans and all life. The darker Sagittarius may allow her instinctive generosity and good nature to become the tool of her ego. The challenge is always there for all Sagittarians to use their generosity for the right purposes. Giving ought never to be about ego, but it can become a temptation too great for some of them.

She may be far-sighted and visionary, idealistic and inspirational—but a Sagittarius in the grip of her ego can become an over-inflated, opinionated know-it-all. Yes, she is usually smart, her intellect is broad and sharp, and she is never stingy about sharing her knowledge—but the dark side of that is a tendency to wax lyrical too often and too enthusiastically. Sagittarian Moons can be guilty of this as well, since emotionally they have a great need to share their truth. It can be hard for Sagittarians to see that their truth is not necessarily *the* truth.

For all that, light or dark, if you or your partner is gifted with Sagittarian energy, life is going to be an adventure in the true sense of the word. Of all the signs, Sagittarius is most about adventure. The territories you will explore (whether by choice or because you've been dragged along) will include those of the heart and mind, as well as the geography of the planet. Knowing the dark bits will hopefully help you handle your arrow-shooting lover. Deflate where there is overinflation, bring in caution where there is recklessness. Listen, but find your own truth.

Compatibility

The fire signs are naturally compatible with Sagittarius. But again, the "Sun sign matches" are generalizations only—and much depends on the connections between your individual charts. However, generally speaking, Aries and Leo blend their energies well with Sagittarius. There is plenty of outgoing, adventurous spirit in the partnership to keep it fueled.

The earth and water signs don't fare quite so well. Earth can be too stuck in practicality for outgoing Sagittarius, and the centaur is frustrated by water's emotionalism. Sagittarius gets impatient with overemotionalism, and caring and sympathy are not his forte. Water needs to feel nurtured on an emotional level—so this can create some challenges.

The air signs are generally positive matches for Sagittarius: air fans fire's flames. Gemini can work well with Sagittarius, being its opposite sign (they have much in common)—all the better if there is compatibility around their respective Moons.

Relationship Clues

Allow your Sagittarian partner the freedom to pursue his or her unique path in life. Being tied down, in any way, is toxic to the Sagittarian soul. It is true, Sagittarius, like all of us, must learn the balance between freedom and the responsibilities of a committed partnership—but you will help your relationship most by being the bigger one here. You can do this by seeing that the impulse to explore, to travel, to start something new, is not a rejection of you, but purely something that comes from deep within, and that something is the urge for soul expansion.

If you decide to expand your own center by journeying with your Sagittarius, all the better. If she excludes you, or you don't need or want to be part of where she is moving to, then be large of heart and graciously allow your lover to do what she needs to do. You will be rewarded if you can be that person in this relationship. Sagittarius needs to feel he is not tied down; even if he is married, he still wants to feel he can fly on a whim and do his own thing. Neediness does not sit well with this sign—so you are going to have to grow up in this relationship. Expanding your own mental horizons through learning new things can be a great boon to your relationship with a Sagittarius. You will automatically become more interesting, and that translates to an invitation to find a new meaning for Sagittarius. There is nothing he loves more.

Another thing—optimism can be learned. If you feel down, think up. The ability to see the silver lining and be positive, even through the tough times, will make this relationship one your Sagittarian lover will never want to leave.

Capricorn

Capricorn the Light

The soul taking on a life with the Sun in Capricorn has the intention of learning integrity. This is the lifetime of full-fledged, responsible adulthood. Coming to a realization of the power of control and self-discipline, the Capricorn Sun is here to experience the rewards of a commitment to a "great work."

The highest moral integrity, inner fortitude, and resilience enable this soul to shoulder heavy burdens. This is his mission. This is a lifetime to measure progress and determination in terms of worldly success. Capricorn's element, earth, and mode of expression, cardinal, combine the strength of energy with endurance. The Capricorn soul has his feet on the ground, and his eyes are focused on the higher road. He is capable of great achievement in this lifetime because he understands intuitively the unity of the physical and the spiritual. He knows the power of investing heart and soul in the cause of worldly achievement.

As if to counter the unrestrained optimism and adventurous spirit of Sagittarius, Capricorn brings to the evolutionary cycle the phase of seriousness. The soul in the Capricorn incarnation is done with philosophy and finding the meaning of life; he is interested now only in translating that awareness into his "great work." His life is going to be a monument to his achievement—however he chooses to translate the word.

The goat is an earth sign and a yin sign, so the feeling is introverted and somewhat negative; there is a sense of being burdened that Capricorn carries around. This is because the goat is concerned with excellence; and more than that, he is aware of the necessity of the work involved to reach that level of mastery. Ambition is a keyword for Capricorn—but it is important to understand that this is about his great work. It is not an overinflated ego's ambition to be someone in the world. It is more a soul yearning to create something in the world.

Capricorn is on a mission in this life to produce a great work of some description. Ambition doesn't necessarily mean a material ambition, as in becoming financially "successful." It can show itself in a drive to overcome difficult circumstances, poverty perhaps, and raise a successful family. It may be some great quest: to climb a mountain (classically symbolic for the sign of the goat), or to be captain of a sports team. The point is: there is a drive, an urge to advance oneself by creating something great!

This is the positive side of this serious sign. Excellence, mastery, perfection. All "masters" walk a Capricornian road. The ultimate destination of Capricorn is mastery—and there is no reaching it without hard work, discipline, practice, and effort. The sign is ruled by Saturn, and this planet is known as a hard taskmaster. It has rulership over the laws of the physical universe and all material forms—and here lies another insight to the Capricorn psyche.

Advancement is important to Capricorn because of its physical or material connotations. With improved status and prestige, and with the advancement and recognition on all levels generally comes greater wealth—and wealth brings a level of material security in this third dimension.

To have what we want is riches, but to be able to do without is power.
—George MacDonald

This is where the higher Capricorn can shine most brightly. The goat is unafraid of hard work and is usually highly self-disciplined. The inner voice of Saturn is a tough one, and it constantly impels its natives to better themselves. He will be the one studying late into the night for that next degree, working hours after everyone else has gone home, practicing long and hard and plowing through his weekends with homework and accomplishing the physical tasks necessary for an ordered life. All of this can add up to a lonely road. Pleasure and enjoyment may be sacrificed on the altar of achievement—and it's a sacrifice that can lead to isolation. Not many understand this drive, or want to be around the determination and seriousness of one who does. But it is a price Capricorn is usually willing to pay.

If you are in a relationship with a Capricorn native, then, don't be offended and don't take it personally that he will seemingly place greater importance on work than on you. The goat just can't help it. It is that deep inner compulsion to be better, to advance, to become more secure in the world. Your lover is a disciplined achiever, and that means he won't be the one to suggest lying in bed late on a Saturday morning, and it might take quite a bit of persuasion from you to keep him there.

Capricorn is a very good planner. The goat has an innate understanding of the skills required to accomplish a task. Time management is one of the fortes of this sign that knows, above all others, how to organize itself within the structures of time and the limitations of rules and laws. Capricorn's ruler, Saturn, is also known as Father Time (and the Grim Reaper, who cuts down everything in the physical world in the fullness of time), so we would expect individuals with Capricorn strong in their charts (Sun-sign Capricorns) to understand the limitations of time better than anyone else. This is one of the reasons Capricorn is often found at the top of organizations; she has a deep knowledge of what needs to be done and how to do it most effectively and efficiently. Capricorn is the boss more often than not. She is ordered, organized, shrewd, strategic, systematic, thorough, and painstaking.

While those qualities might not sound very romantic, at the heart of this physical life lies the necessity for all of those things. Without order, without discipline and the limitations of boundaries and responsibilities, chaos reigns. Chaos filters through to every aspect of life—even our relationships, if we are not careful to keep it in check through self-discipline. A person who is capable of leading an organization is innately equipped to bring that same disciplined approach to all his relationships. But when it comes to the romantic ones, he may just need a little guidance.

Capricorn is an earth sign, and the earth signs have that dogged determination and ability to persevere and persist long after the other signs have thrown in the towel. What this means in relationships is that with good communication, you have here the raw material needed to design and create the relationship you want. Your Capricorn lover will listen to appeals to her sense of logic. Both sexes have a very deep sense of commitment. Capricorn, once set on a course of action, is not easily swayed from it. And this includes relationships. Very rarely is the goat the one to quit on a relationship, once he or she has made a commitment.

You may need to put aside the urge toward wild displays of emotional pleading, because this won't work as well as calm and measured suggestions as to how things could be done better. You will need to appeal to his sense of "getting somewhere"—and don't waste too much time in doing so. It might seem calculating and lacking in spontaneity (which it is), but your Capricorn partner will be happier and more likely to please you if you can somehow formalize your "relationship desires." Put them in writing. Draw up a proposal.

Plans for holidays and weekend breaks, it is true, you may have to come up with (if you don't, you run the risk of your Capricorn sneaking back to work on Sunday afternoon). But if you take the initiative and present your ideas in a thorough, no-nonsense sort of way, you are more likely to get what you want. If you get all emotional over the fact he never spends any time with you—and his complete lack of romanticism—you can probably expect not much to change. Your mountain goat is on a mission to advance himself in this life; and much as he loves you, he doesn't really understand the importance of human relations. You have to be his teacher and appeal to his nature—which is only happy when his external world is ordered. Try to help him see that it is an achievement to have a successful relationship, and talk about the ingredients of such an entity together.

Once you understand this, life can be very secure with Capricorn—not to mention very comfortable, a big plus for the hours of hard work he has invested along the way.

Capricorn needs to feed its inner Sun through devotion to a great discipline. This soul needs to feel the deep satisfaction of achievement, to stay focused on the goal and steadily work toward it.

> *They wait, when they should turn to journeys,*
> *They stiffen, when they should bend.*
> —Louise Bogan

What feeds the spirit of the Capricorn Sun is the knowledge he has the power and the endurance to acquire whatever he needs in the world. The path of mastery is open to this soul—and to feel alive in the world, to feel vitalized and energized, he is wise to choose such a path. But in choosing this path, he must balance the persistence and discipline it requires with healthy doses of heart. He needs to love and be loved. Work feeds his solar function, but love and relationships are vital to balance the excess mental and physical strain he puts on himself. The great work for this soul is anything capable of leading to mastery. Finding this path and staying on it is soul food, fueling the life force of the Capricorn Sun.

Capricorn the Dark

Intentions, and not feelings, are at the root of Capricorn's actions in the world. The goat has this deep and unswerving commitment to seeing things through and realizing, or making manifest in the material world, his aims and ambitions. He does this through hard work, perseverance, and discipline. It is action that counts, and Capricorn knows this with every molecule of his being. Feelings, bah humbug, there is not enough time for them; they distract from the real business of living—which is getting on with things: things that are real, that is. Intention, action, achievement—those three words could sum up the essential modus operandi of the goat.

Time, every one of them knows, is of the essence. With Capricorn there can be a sense of pressure because of a feeling of time running out, or there not being enough of it to accomplish what needs accomplishing. This can be a most difficult thing to live with. You just want to say, "Chill, relax, let it go" . . . But she can't. Her intentions rule, and she needs time to make them happen. Feelings, they are an inconvenience usually—and so the goat deals with them by doing the obvious thing: ignoring them.

That should have sent up a flash of warning, if you are in a relationship with the goat. Ignore feelings—sacrilege! Especially if you are a water sign. We ignore feelings at our peril. Capricorn's deep sense of commitment and ability to persevere is paramount in relationship. However, the flip side, the dark side of this commitment, is that this intensity of purpose may be a rigid suppression of emotional involvement. Capricorn excels at this. No other sign is better at controlling its emotions than Capricorn. Natives of this sign will suppress their emotional life if it seems to oppose or create obstacles on the road they are on. With her unsurpassed self-discipline and excessively developed work ethic, she is more than capable of shutting out the voice of her heart and focusing her energy on her ambitious goals.

Some darker Capricorns, however, fail completely to realize the essence of the sign's deep need for responsibility, achievement, and a strong work ethic. They prefer to escape from the onerous business of working for a living, and these are the ones who fall prey to addictions—they become completely irresponsible. These are the very dark Capricorns and are the minority.

It can be ultimately self-destructive to deny (however he does it) the emotional side of his nature, but many a Capricorn will not realize he is harming himself until it is too late. Others will withdraw from him as he seems to enclose himself in a shell of self-imposed authority. "I shall be like that tree, I shall die at the top," said Jonathan Swift—and this, sadly, can be the fate of many a Capricorn too enmeshed in his drives to recognize the essential meaning of life. He may be the richest, the most powerful, the top of the heap—but is he the happiest? The sacrifices he has made to get to the top eventually come back to haunt him. Self-containment, like any "virtue" when taken too far, can become destructive. Studies have shown the benefits to health of being in a loving relationship, and of having loving connections with others. Without these, our life force dwindles and our physical body winds up in a state of disease.

One of the sacrifices of Capricorn's quest to get to the top is the dimming of the natural spark of emotional expression—the spark that links heart to heart, body to body. Too rigidly controlling, the mountain goat on this path eventually becomes incapable of any level of emotional expression because the life force has been all used up in the thrust to get ahead and survive—no, thrive—in the physical world. Yes, it is true he may have relationships—after a fashion. But these will lack the passion and fire of spontaneity, vulnerability, and deep merging that are the hallmarks of true intimacy.

The mountain goat who has been on the long, hard slog to the top for many years can find himself at a place where he is the victim of his own unwillingness to engage his feelings, and that place can be a very lonely one.

Capricorn needs, then, to re-learn how to engage. If your lover is born under the sign of the goat, you are pivotal to his well-being and there is nothing for it but for you to be his teacher here. He probably won't get it on his own, because he is too consumed, as we've seen, with progress. Relationships, he thinks, ought to take care of themselves. But as we know, they don't. They take nurturing and care and lots of loving attention. We cannot expect to spend every waking hour focused on work and have relationships that last the distance, or even bring satisfaction in the short term.

So what would teaching your Capricorn lover require? Looking at the dark side of the Capricorn soul, the message in a nutshell is this: your goat needs to learn a new discipline—that is, the discipline of sharing herself emotionally. If it can be explained to her in this way, that emotional skills are just another discipline we all need to acquire, the initial resistance can be more easily broken down. Problems in intimate relationships usually start with one single factor: a lack of awareness. People are just not aware of the skills they need to develop to create a successful relationship. With Capricorn, the most important of those skills is that of sharing emotionally. The tendency is to shut down and repress feelings because they appear to Capricorn to be derailers, throwing him off course from the essential business of getting ahead. But if he doesn't want to die lonely and alone, then he needs some help.

The goat has a hard exterior, but the inside story is in marked contrast. It is invariably fear that drives Capricorn onward and upward in life. With Saturn as his ruler, fear is never far away. Fear and insecurity underlie the drive to escape them through the insulation of material wealth and/or achievement. Or, as we saw with the particularly dark Capricorn, through addictions. But what Capricorn needs to learn is to recognize what she really wants and then to ask for it! If she can be helped to see that it is fear that keeps her protecting her feelings by burying them and focusing on the tangibles in life, then she can overcome her demons by facing them. She needs to understand that it is her connections to others that will give her the security she craves.

She is not really an island, or a rock, but a deeply emotional, heart-ruled human being who needs, above all else, loving connections with others.

Loving a Capricorn is not difficult once you understand the inner workings of the character. There will be times, and probably many of them, when you will have little option but to get on with your own life while your partner directs the majority of his energies toward his goals. But in between, encouraging him to be less self-contained, more expressive of his feelings, and more conscious of them in the first place can make life comfortable, safe, and deeply loving. And don't forget: you have a partner here who will go the long haul with you, come hell or high water—and that, in these times, is a lot to be grateful for.

Compatibility

Fellow earth signs are natural matches with Capricorn. They *get* the drive of the sign to make things work on a material level.

Capricorn can be altogether too serious for the fire signs, and not sufficiently mentally stimulating for air.

However, as with all Sun sign matches, the most vital thing is the linkage of all planets and sensitive points in your respective birth charts. Incompatible Suns can work well, if they are supported by harmonious Moon and Ascendant signs.

The water signs, notwithstanding what was said before about emotionalism (or lack thereof on the part of the goat), can work well. There is a very grounding, real quality to Capricorn that the water signs find attractive. Water often has enough emotionalism for two. And Capricorn, too, is attracted to what he finds mysterious and puzzling; the water signs have an affinity with the world of feelings, and that world is quite a puzzle to the goat. What we lack in ourselves we seek in a partner, and nowhere is this more evident than when Capricorn partners with a water sign.

Relationship Clues

Having the awareness of your Capricorn partner's underlying belief that he needs to work hard and get ahead in life will help you soften toward him. Even when he is being hard, stern, and overly authoritarian, open your heart and give him some loving in response, if you can; you will be giving more than you know. This is because the natural instinct is toward closing down when we are confronted by an overly authoritarian person. When we are disregarded, criticized, or spoken severely to, our hearts shrink. If you can see your Capricorn partner is doing it, not to hurt you but because he is afraid to trust life to support him, you can show him another way. That way is a balancing of his admirable skills and ability to work long and hard combined with a trust in life. The result is high integrity. Tell him that when you give value to the universe, it gives value to you. In other words, he is deserving of the rewards and they will come his way. But he must learn to listen to his soul. He shuts it out too readily, in his drive to work the material world. Help him to listen to the softer side, to go into the world of his feelings.

The only way to have a friend is to be one.
—Ralph Waldo Emerson

Capricorn can shut out her sensitivities to soul-shifting experiences—music, romance, and intimacy—in her quest to secure her place on the world's stage. But you, as her partner, can help her reconnect with that part of herself she is denying. Capricorn needs relationship more than she knows—and you may have to be the one to show her this.

———— *Aquarius* ————

Aquarius the Light

We come to a phase in the evolutionary cycle where all that has gone before has brought the soul to a place where it sees true. Aquarius understands the human condition, and accepts unconditionally all it comprises. The sign of the water bearer is the sign of the humanitarian and the awakener.

The element of air ignites the higher mind—the intuitive capacity. Aquarius belongs to the fixed modality, so air is stabilized, unyielding, determined. Rational thinking and intellectualizing that go beyond the "normal" mind are Aquarius' domain. Gifts of higher thinking and intuition come from ruler Uranus' link to the collective mind.

The soul choosing an Aquarian Sun for this sojourn in the earthly realms has the intention, the endpoint, of understanding the balance of individuality and sociability. Independence and space must be married to the need to share, to be part of society, to be in relationship. Never an easy road to walk, the soul of the Aquarian Sun has all it needs to achieve such a balance.

Believing deeply in personal freedom, the Aquarius soul is on a mission to share its universalistic perspective with others, and to liberate them from old and inhibiting ways of thinking.

Aquarius is the rebel, the mover, and the shaker, intent on dismantling the status quo—however quietly. He is iconoclastic, original, innovative. His ruler is the planet symbolic of the collective higher mind, of rebellion and innovation, Uranus. He has a direct linkage to the universal mind, translating as a spot-on intuition. Aquarius is an air sign and a fixed sign; he lives in the world of thought, and he is resistant to change. He is conventional when it suits, and at the same time startlingly unconventional.

As we've seen, each sign compensates for (and encompasses) the sign preceding it. Where Capricorn was obsessively concerned with authority and discipline, Aquarius is innately anti-authoritarian, and believes only in self-responsibility. Responsibility has been learned in the Capricorn phase, and now Aquarius wants to take that and expand it. The broadness of view of Aquarius is its gift, but sometimes its curse. Because natives of the sign see so readily beyond the limitations of normal social protocols, their desire to do things differently, to liberate themselves and others from the restrictions of the status quo, can result in feeling cut off or detached from others. And at other times, Aquarius chooses to detach herself; in fact, she needs to. Space feeds her inner Sun. Isolationism is one of the crosses Aquarius seems fated to bear, in her quest to reveal a more holistic vision and to liberate humanity from the bonds of external control.

Aquarius is the opposite sign to Leo; and so where Leo is concerned with the ego, approval, and validation, Aquarius is so completely other, 180 degrees departed. This gives Aquarians the freedom to do as they please, because they are completely unconcerned with what others think of them.

There is a deep vein of unconventionality that runs through every Aquarius. These people are the oddballs of the zodiac; the eccentric, absent-minded professor archetype is Aquarian. They trip through life, not fully aware of what is going on around them—so consumed are they in their own thought processes.

Aquarius is the last of the air signs. But where the other air signs, Gemini and Libra, are concerned with personal and social thinking, Aquarius takes the mind to a whole new dimension, the universal. The abstract is the domain of Uranus, Aquarius' ruler—a transpersonal planet associated with revolution, liberation, change, reform, progress, innovation, genius, and awakening. Natives of Aquarius readily embody this impulse to awaken others. Awakenings often come through shock; if you are in a relationship with Aquarius, you will probably know the raw feeling, as if you've been hit in the stomach, that comes in the wake of an Aquarian "truth-telling" episode. This individual will awaken you to aspects of yourself like no other!

Thinking about the meaning of the symbol for Aquarius, a supernal being pouring water from an open-ended vessel, we can feel the essence of the sign, and witness it in every Aquarius we encounter. The open-ended vessel symbolizes universal consciousness pouring down from heaven to earth—with humanity as the container, or holder, of this consciousness or wisdom. When you truly know Aquarians, you know this is where they come from. They instinctively feel themselves to be holders of a higher awareness or consciousness—and they see their job as being dispensers of this wisdom; they feel compelled to share it and thereby awaken and enlighten others. The truth of the matter is: because Aquarians do have this ability to see true, they invariably hit the nail on the head.

One of the spin-offs of this sense of responsibility to awaken others is the feeling of separateness or detachment most Aquarians live with. When you see things others cannot, it is difficult to "be one of them"; so, like Capricorn, the Aquarian road can be a lonely one. The reasons are very different, however. Capricorn's loneliness comes from its relentless pursuit of achievement and ambition; Aquarius' comes from a more abstract dimension—the relinquishment of ego, and feeling misunderstood and detached from humanity as a whole.

If you are in a relationship with an Aquarius, you will know about detachment. You will know it well. At times it is quite tangible. It can manifest as a physical detachment, a "disappearing act," or as a psychological one, as in closing off from you. If she has been hurt over something you did or said, she can simply "cut out." She may disappear for days at a time, because Aquarius needs time to process what has happened. Being so intellectually oriented, everything is filtered (again and again) through the mind. Often the water bearer will drive herself nuts with the relentless analysis and re-analysis that she seems unable to stop. Unlike the water signs, who feel the emotion and act in response to it, Aquarius feels and then dissects mentally—then acts. So there is a time lag—and nothing can be done about it. You just have to wait for your wacky partner to re-emerge, and she will only do it when she's ready. These things can't be rushed. The insights that emerge from the period of detachment are usually worth waiting for.

If he first disappeared on you in a childish huff, saying some hurtful things (in his own defense, of course), leaving you alone—for days if he so chooses—he will come back, when he is ready, with a far more mature response. Know that you cannot decide when to connect, or reconnect, with your Aquarian; that lightning mind of his, linked by a strong tie to his heart, has its own agenda. No amount of persuasion will bring him back if he is not ready to reconnect with you. It may feel like punishment; it may feel painful—but if you can recognize that this is something your Aquarius needs to do, to feed his solar function (and so come back to his aliveness), that he needs to detach from everything and everyone from time to time—then you can relax and let go. Allow him to take his time. Uranus energy operates on a different timeline from the rest of the planets; it even spins in a different way. Everything about this planet is unusual.

It is unusual to crave social interaction and almost simultaneously shun it, to feel alone in the midst of company. But however we look at it, the fact remains that Aquarians somehow, some way, end up in their own space.

This seeming negative has come under the light side of the sign. The reason is that everything about Uranus is unpredictable. It is the planet responsible for shocks and surprises. It is always waking us up with surprise, and so it may be surprising to find this aspect of the Aquarian character under the light side—when, logically, it could just as easily fit under the dark side. Certainly, if your partner is an Aquarius, his detachment and his disappearing act can feel very dark when you're on the receiving end of it. But a little more thought reveals a higher insight. Detachment offers a gift in relationship. It allows space, room to breathe. And most powerfully of all, in his absence, the water bearer assimilates all sides of the argument. He sees your perspective. Only time and space can deliver up such an overview.

So don't resent the strange and detached ways of your Aquarian lover. Know that when he returns, he will be centered once again. He needs that space to honor the Uranian urge to stand apart and feel the truth of a situation—in splendid isolation.

No other sign is more socially conscious, more genuinely concerned and caring for others, or so unfalteringly allowing of every nuance of the human condition. If you are in a relationship with an Aquarian, you may know that on some level, all and everything will be forgiven. Your Aquarian partner outshines all the other signs combined when it comes to "eating humble pie." This is because of his absence of ego involvement. He simply recognizes the fallibility of human nature and accommodates himself to it. His natural detachment helps here, too—he is able to shift himself away from the situation sufficiently to allow understanding to filter through.

This is not to say that these people are complete pushovers—far from it, in fact. They can be as judgmental as the next person (though they'd be horrified to hear that), but they are usually able, given sufficient time for thoughtfulness, to move beyond ego and see the bigger picture. Even when they are so clearly the wounded party, they will forgive. But they will not forget. To forget would be to ignore the lessons, and Aquarius is very conscious of the evolutionary nature of life, the intention of life lessons; these people are very good at "getting it"—eventually. They will not ignore you or seek revenge, but they will move on. Life, they know, is about progress—and there is no going back once Aquarius has been wounded. So you have been warned. It might seem as though all is forgiven, and in a sense it is, because Aquarius understands your human weakness—but lose their trust, and things will never be the same again.

It needs to be said that for all that, Aquarius does have a remarkable capacity to shoulder hurts and slights. Again, it is this higher perspective coming to the fore—and the absence of ego control. So while it may feel at times as if the person you are in a relationship with, your Aquarius, sees you as one of the group, if you truly have captured an Aquarian heart, you have devotion, loyalty, understanding, and a love that transcends (and includes) the personal. And those add up to something precious.

Aquarius needs to feed its inner Sun through seeking the balance between the personal and the collective. This soul needs to have its life force replenished by mixing with like minds, communicating, and being social. But it needs, equally, to create space. The Aquarian soul needs mental space to assimilate the learning it has absorbed from "the group." To do so means it needs to periodically move away from others physically and emotionally. The inner Sun, the life force, is vitalized and energized by social interaction and freedom to express its uniqueness. The Aquarian soul is truly unique.

Love is only chatter,
Friends are all that matter.
—Gelett Burgess

Aquarius the Dark

"Love is only chatter, friends are all that matter." This quote from art-ist (and Aquarian) Gelett Burgess illuminates the Aquarian approach to love and relationships so well. Why? Simply because Aquarius represents the principle of agape, or brotherly love; friends then are as important (in many cases more so!) as lovers. This is a love that is universalistic: loving another simply because he or she is human. Personal love is a trickier thing for the water bearer—and this can be their undoing.

Because Aquarius is such an original thinker—the archetypal eccentric, mad scientist, rebel, and genius rolled into one—the stan-dard themes of love and relationships, those scripts written by the patriarchal forbears of our society, are somehow difficult to swallow for her. Remember, Aquarius is not a rule follower. To the contrary, the water bearer wants to write her own rules, and she wants every-one else to have the same freedom. In many of life's avenues, this is all fine and good. The Aquarius energy is responsible for many of our greatest social advances. New Zealand, an Aquarius Sun country, was the first to give women the vote, the first to introduce social welfare. And not to forget New Zealander Sir Edmund Hillary, the first person to climb Mt. Everest. The Aquarius energy is always avant-garde, always ahead of the crowd. When it comes to the heart, the rules society has written had good reasoning behind them in the era in which they were written. For instance, monogamy ensures (or intended to) that the genetic lineage of a child is accounted for. It kept everything so much tidier. But we are now moving into a new consciousness, and Aquarius, being the trendsetter at the forefront of every new movement, is, as always, ahead of its time.

In actual fact, in matriarchal societies prior to the rise of the patriarchy, there was no need for such rules as monogamy—they didn't exist.

The water bearer doesn't want the rules that someone else wrote to apply to her. The idea of one committed, prioritized love, then, is not likely to come naturally to her. The conditioning most of us have absorbed from our society seems to have conveniently passed right on by all Aquarians. Actually, she does struggle with the whole thing sometimes. If you are in a relationship with an Aquarius, you may know this pain well: the pain of feeling that everyone else (a friend, usually—everyone is a "friend" to Aquarius) matters just as much (at times more!) to your lover than you do. The idea of prioritization, when it comes to people, is a difficult one for your average water bearer.

When Aquarius slips further into the dark side, this problem intensifies. The obvious implication is an inability to commit. But this may not necessarily be the issue. Many natives of the sign of the water bearer commit quite readily. It is afterwards that the rot sets in. Being exclusive with anyone is just not on the agenda as far as Aquarius is concerned, so unless the partner is pretty independent and able to make a life for herself outside the relationship, things can turn bleak. The point is, commitment to an Aquarius does not mean the same thing as it does to most people. To an Aquarian, a marriage commitment, for example, does not mean that he cannot go out with his friends, that he cannot prioritize his work or his colleagues. He won't think twice about working late and then having a few drinks before coming home. If he's been away on a business trip, it won't occur to him to go straight home after work on his first night back. No, not at all; there is a social gathering happening with work people, and that, it seems, is where he most wants to be.

All of this can be very wounding to the Aquarian partner. The prognosis for long-term success is not fantastic when this darker side of the sign prevails too much, because usually the point is reached where the partner looks elsewhere for that intimacy. (I'm not talking sex here; I'm talking emotional intimacy.)

What needs to occur for this water bearer is an "awakening." Aquarius is about the business of revelation and enlightening others to new possibilities, but there comes a time when they need a dose of their own medicine. This can come through the shock of a betrayal or divorce. Perhaps the shock needn't be on quite that level, but something needs to occur to make the Aquarian native realize that while it is all very good and well oiling the social wheels of society, it is in the realms of her most intimate partnership that her energies need to be directed occasionally. At least, if she wants to have a relationship, that is.

The intricacies of intimate relationships are not instinctively understood when Aquarius is strong in one's nature. If you are in a relationship with a native of this sign, then you will need to communicate your needs. Aquarius is an air sign, remember, and so these people relate to words and ideas. If you sit in wounded silence, he will never get it. He will blissfully continue on, the life of the party, charming everyone within earshot, involving himself in social causes and sports groups and clubs and organizations of all sorts. It will just not occur to him that you might need something more out of your partnership. That sitting home alone night after night, and seeing him for half the weekend at best, is just not enough for you.

I'm sorry, but it will be up to you. You will need to communicate and keep on communicating until the penny finally drops. It may take a while. And you don't want to be a nag—so you will have to be subtle. What you need to communicate is the pain that your water bearer is unconsciously causing you through his or her neglect.

That means not accusing—but rather, as rationally as possible, conveying the impact this frequent absence is having on you. It is very much an unconscious neglect, because on another level, no sign is more faithful and loyal. And this is important. The urge for personal space is so strong that Aquarius simply, instinctively, sets out to do as he pleases—and what pleases him is to be socially involved in life.

It is important to remember that the social involvements Aquarius makes are generally nonsexual. Aquarius is interested in universal love ahead of personal love—that's the bottom line. Thus, fidelity is generally a given. Unfaithfulness is more of the nonintimate (universal) kind, but it is an unfaithfulness of time and energy—both of which are needed to support and nurture a relationship.

I'd like to suggest getting out and having a life of your own, creating your own social agenda. But this really is just papering over the holes. It won't work. Underneath, the resentment will build and you will get no closer to creating the intimacy you want. Yes, to a point making a life outside the relationship will be important. Aquarius values independence—so clingy partners are not the ideal for this sign. But the real issue is helping your partner grow in awareness. Every relationship needs priority time, and this cannot just be once a week or when there is nothing else pressing going on. Every moment a choice is made to put the needs of someone or something else—work, friends, the group—ahead of the relationship can be another nail in the coffin.

Aquarius needs to be told. If you don't, who will? The universe in the form of an "awakening" tactic, that's who. And what a waste of a good partner! They will try again, because there is a lot of love in those hearts of theirs. They may make the same mistake again. Aquarius is a fixed element sign—which means these people can be very rigid in their thinking, very persistent and inflexible in their patterns and responses. But if you truly love that Aquarius, you don't have to settle for being one of the gang. Gently and sensitively tell him that you need him to put you first. When a woman knows she's number one, she can create a relationship strong enough and passionate enough to last a lifetime. (I guess that goes for a man, too.) If she has to fight for that position, which sadly many partners of Aquarians do, a "lesser" side of her nature can manifest itself. Darkness can creep into the relationship that began so brightly. Aquarian women, by the way, are no different. Their partners, usually men, may be able to handle that nature a little more easily than most women do.

To close on a more positive note: Aquarius, with its lightning quick insightfulness and ability to tune in to the reality of others, has the greatest potential to be a lover of the universal and the intimate. Usually after a shock or two in the relationship department, this man or woman is capable of creating a partnership that is a unique combination of deep intimacy, personal freedom, and a generous and open-hearted connection with fellow planet dwellers. That could be worth the pain and the energy it may take to achieve.

Compatibility

The usual formula would say the other air signs are most compatible with Aquarius, followed by the fire signs—with the earth and water signs not faring so well. But with Aquarius, like everything with unpredictable Uranus, there are no rules.

In theory, the above should stand true, but in practice you will find Aquarius partnering strongly with Pisces (theoretically not a good match). Such a relationship can be above and beyond, in every way, Aquarius' partnerships with the other air signs—or fire signs, for that matter. In the case of Pisces, there seems to be an above-average linkage of these two signs. They are the last signs of the zodiac, and both universal signs. Often there is an attraction between adjacent signs, and for Aquarius, it is likely that the calm, passive, sensitive, and humanitarian nature of Pisces is balm for their overly active minds and equally humanitarian souls. They are both ruled by the outer planets, so the linkage seems to be "beyond this world." It breaks all the rules, and it goes deep into soul territory.

As always, the most essential aspect of compatibility between the Sun signs is the compatibility of the charts of the individuals as a whole. But in general the signs Libra and Gemini are the most positive matches with Aquarius, although remember that too much of a good thing can be a bad thing. If you are a fire sign, things can work well with Aquarius, as freedom is an underlying principle for you both. If you are an earth sign, the universe has some learning in store for you, which you probably will not be able to avoid. Clearly, you have come together to resolve some old, unfinished business.

Relationship Clues

The greatest gift you can bring to a relationship with an Aquarius is tolerance of his need to have a life outside of your relationship. Yes, it can hurt to realize you are not number one in this man's life. The remedy is to meet your own needs—and this is true for everyone in a relationship, not just those in a relationship with a water bearer. We burden our relationship too much when we impose our security needs. You will best ensure the survival of your relationship, then, by understanding, deeply, that your partner's need to be with others is not about you in any way. It is simply that she needs to circulate and communicate (air sign, remember: communication is important) with many members of the human family. Doing so feeds her solar function. You can and you should convey your feelings on this, but you should also try to accept it. If it hurts you too much, you owe it to the both of you to tell her that you don't feel good when she goes for coffee with the guy she works with—even if she is doing it to help him sort out his marital difficulties.

When we are in a relationship, we have an obligation to mind our p's and q's, and that means to alter behaviors that hurt our partners. With Aquarius, it is your job to let your partner know what is acceptable and what isn't. The world of "other people" can be the cross you have to bear in this relationship, but it is a cross you can dilute with compassionate communication.

The positive of that is: you have a partner who is fully tuned in to the human condition, and has an ability to be larger of heart than anyone else you know.

—————————— *Pisces* ——————————

Pisces the Light

When a soul has entered the Pisces cycle of incarnation, much learning has been done; there is profound passivity born of understanding life and the human condition. The Pisces soul has made at least one long trek through all the signs of the zodiac and has reached a point where it knows the limitations of the flesh and seeks a union with something higher. It is ready to let go. Pisces wants to transcend the human experience and become part of a more divine reality.

The endpoint for Pisces is identification with consciousness—egoic and universal consciousness. The attainment of "individuation" is the intention. Individuation comes from fully realizing the separate, ego consciousness and taking this into the cosmic ocean: transcending the little self for the larger Self.

Ethereal Neptune, symbolic of the cosmic ocean, rules Pisces. Neptune impels humans to swim in the ocean of universal consciousness, to be as One. It urges those who resonate with its frequency, the Pisces Suns especially, to escape the mundane realm of living in the density of the third dimension and takes them to a more refined place, where glamour, illusion, fantasy, and artistic creativity bring heart and soul to the fore, where the sacred is honored.

Life is not only a physical journey, it is a spiritual one. The soul experiencing life with a Pisces Sun knows this, through every molecule of its being.

Pisceans come into the world with an innate understanding of the thread that unites all of life. Here is the origin of the sensitivity and compassion of this deeply feeling water sign. Unlike Cancerian sensitivity, Pisces sensitivity is imbued with a universal perspective, so it is more empathetic, less acutely subjective. The fish feels others' pain so deeply because its boundaries are fluid. It understands the interconnectedness of all life, the nature of the One. It is all one amorphous, all-inclusive, undifferentiated whole.

Neptune symbolizes unity consciousness, transcendence, oneness, sacrifice, surrender, nonattachment and selfless love. The love of the masters and saints. These are the essence of the Piscean soul, the potential open to it. And there is poison, too—beckoning this sensitive child of sea god Neptune. Pisces is offered two pathways: to swim upstream, to life, or to drift down, to stagnant waters.

Being in love with a Pisces can be a sublime, transcendent, romantic, and totally unifying experience. This partner will take you to places you never knew existed, because the fish knows that real love is a soul-to-soul connection. It is this you will touch with a Piscean partner—the part of you that transcends the physical. For love to last, for Pisces, this connection on a soul level is vital. Without it, something inside shrivels up and dies. Many a fish has resorted to the wine bottle, or worse, when love like this has gone—or if it never came in the first place. Lost souls they can become, adrift in the sea of life, passive, yielding, open to being abused and used, victims of their own infinite hearts.

> *It is only with the heart that one can see rightly; what is essential is invisible to the eye.*
> —Antoine de Saint-Exupéry

Pisceans with stronger backbones do it differently. They keep seeking—knowing that such a love is their God-given birthright. They are not content to settle for less. It has to be a soul connection, or nothing. These are the fish who swim upstream. The ones who use the wisdom born of a long trek through all the signs, and their own unique understanding of the Infinite, to create relationships and lives that truly blend the best of the spiritual and the material.

Being in a relationship with a higher Pisces can be an otherworld experience. In fact, most of the time your partner will seem to be from beyond this world. There is an enchantment, a magical quality to Pisceans when they reveal themselves in a truly intimate relationship. If they belong to a higher consciousness, they will open their hearts with complete and total willingness—to you and for you. Are you up for it? Not too many are, in fact. The Piscean way of love is of a different nature than that of the other signs, which means it can be challenging. It is imperative for the soul in them to feel the soul in you. Their Suns demand that they do. And believe it, you can't fake that! If you are not in it, heart and soul, as they are, then don't even think of hanging around, trying to have your cake and eat it too. Your Piscean lover will soon be an ex-Piscean lover. The fish, with a flick of her tail, will one day turn around and swim off in a new direction. She knows that there is someone else out there who will love her the way she deserves and needs to be loved. And there is.

But given you are that one, what can you expect and how can you keep that beautiful, ideal state—the one that seemed too good to be true at the start? Well, in many ways it was. Real life, as we all know, even Pisceans know, can undermine and corrode the highest aspirations and cause even the most open hearts to close (temporarily in the case of the more conscious fish; letting go comes naturally to them, as they know that life pain is as transient as everything else in the world).

First and foremost, and probably last as well, the way to hold on to that spiritualized, romantic love is to hold to one thought: love is what you do. Soul connections are strengthened through doing in the real world.

Pisces is so out of this world that action is not something that comes naturally. Passivity is more like it. When you fall deeply in love, it is easy to go with the flow and merge with your lover on all levels, sharing in that Piscean unity and blending of souls. But when the real world starts to knock on the door, you are going to have to be the strong one. Pisces is not so well equipped to deal with real-world stuff. When the lovemaking is over, then, how can you keep that connection alive, and with it, the undying affection of your ocean-dwelling lover?

It is the day-to-day, real-life stuff that will keep your relationship with Pisces alive. Living together, being together through the mundane details of daily life—this is the framework on which the beauty of your soul connection can be hung.

Pick up the phone and see how he is. Tell him you are thinking of him and can't wait to see him again. The male fish are every bit as sensitive as the female, and need constant reassurances that they are loved, that your soul-to-soul connection is still there. Light some candles when you make love, play soothing music, and pour him a glass of wine when he walks in the door.

Bring her flowers—not just when you start dating, but unendingly. See her, hold her, be with her, make a promise to her—and keep it. If you are not a person of your word, then realize you are sowing the seeds of your relationship demise. The fish needs truth when it comes to your intentions and expressions of affection. She senses truth, like no other. And she needs you to act on that truth.

The fish is adept at taking care of the spiritual side of your union, but when it comes to practicalities, she could let you down. That's where she needs you. And I'm not saying she, or he, is not capable of being successful in the "real" world. Did you know there are more billionaires born under Pisces than any other sign? What does that say? My guess is it says the natives of this sign have an innate attunement to the intangibles, to the invisible, out of which everything in the manifest world originates. This attunement enables them to use their consciousness to create, at a high and often successful level, in the material world.

It will help for you to bring your more grounded qualities, practical abilities, and organizational and leadership skills to the mix.

But don't forget the most important thing is your soul-to-soul connection. Your Pisces partner can create the most transcendent connection imaginable between two people on the planet, but she needs to know you are fully, truthfully there with her.

All the signs compensate for the one that went before—and Pisces is making up for the rationality and intellectualizing of Aquarius by coming straight from the heart. Feelings are the beginning, middle, and end with Pisces. Like the water element it belongs to, Pisces blends and molds itself to the surrounding environment and the prevailing emotional climate. The fish takes on the feelings and emotions of everyone around, at times having difficulty establishing where he leaves off and others begin. There is a psychic ability in most Pisceans that means they feel the environment, the moods of others, and even future trends before most of the other signs. It is a mystic-psychic state of consciousness that, like all strengths, can become a weakness if not balanced. Pisces natives need to back up their mystical side with active involvement in the material world.

The excruciating sensitivity of both girl and boy fish means you will need to be very conscious. Too easily wounded—even the higher types; if your Pisces has had her feelings hurt, she can swim off into a dark and deep corner of the pond, simply disappearing on you until she has had a chance to shed her tears and recover her spirits. But it takes a surprisingly small amount of energy to pull her back—she floats easily with the current. A peace offering, an arm around the shoulder, and a heartfelt "I'm sorry" doesn't seem much to ask to have back a connection that will be balm for your world-weary soul whenever you need it.

No one knows how to soothe and comfort like Pisces. But he needs comforting himself, in huge dollops. For all his spiritual insightfulness he can become disoriented and derailed when his feelings are disregarded. The result can be a bit of a mess at times. Such is life, for every positive there's a flip side. The positives of being in an intimate relationship with a Pisces are those that will enrich your spirit, connect you with the sacred, and open your heart—sometimes till it hurts. This is a relationship above and beyond all relationships.

If you are lucky enough to be involved in an intimate relationship with this enigmatic, mystical, at times elusive creature, then you are not only blessed but you have a big responsibility. It is a responsibility to nurture those sensitive feelings and to be courageous enough to go into the emotional depths that only Pisces knows. The rewards, if you do, will be as expansive as they are unfathomable: insights into the ways of your own soul and profound opening of your own heart.

If it is a relationship of the deepest spiritual connection you seek, you could not do better than fall in love with a Pisces. The sons and daughters of Neptune, when playing out their highest evolutionary intent, are the true spirit keepers of the earth.

Go well, and keep your eyes and heart on the river ahead.

Pisces needs to feed its inner Sun through regularly diving into the world of universal consciousness. The deeply spiritual soul who has incarnated with a Pisces Sun needs to immerse in the "other world"— through meditation, music, dance, art, spirituality . . . This soul needs time to retreat from the mundane world and to go within. To feel fully alive, to feel sane in this mad world, the Pisces soul must have regular retreat from it.

Agonies are one of my changes of garments; I do not ask the wounded person how he feels . . . I myself become the wounded person.
—Walt Whitman

Pisces the Dark

The dark side of the Piscean soul holds all the darkness and pain of the eleven that went before—and then some. Where there is potential for enlightenment, for cosmic unity and the bliss of merging with the divine, there is also the potential to slide down into the depths of escapism, depression, and despair. It is no coincidence that the name given to strong alcohol is *spirit*. No other sign has this pull to spirit as strongly as Pisces does. The broken and homeless alcoholic on the street is a manifestation of the Piscean urge to "merge with spirit" gone wrong. There are no shortcuts to any place worth going to—but the fish is highly susceptible to believing there are.

Escape, then, is the downfall of Pisces. Escape from the confines of the mundane world. Escape from the emotional torment of broken love, of abandonment and separation. Original wounds (separation anxiety being foremost of these), which we all have in some measure, seem more acute in the Piscean soul. The desire to escape from them is present from birth. A more conscious Pisces will use this urge to transcend the pull of the material world and create beautiful works of art, music, dance, and literature. Neptune has rulership over these, and his children are the most artistic and creative people on the planet.

On another level, this ability to connect with the divine can be seen in those individuals who work in, and make startling revelations about, the true nature of reality (which is not what we perceive through our three-dimensional glasses). Albert Einstein, scientist and mystic, was a strong Pisces Sun who was able to manifest the highest potentials of the sign.

The lure of the dark side of the sign is ever-present. Pisces, more than any other sign, has this potential to ascend to great heights, and likewise, to fall into the abyss—it is a self-created abyss originating in the desire to transcend the mundane, earthly life. As long as we are in a physical body, there is no escape, no way to get past the constraints of the material world and merge completely into cosmic unity and bliss. The best we can do is catch it in glimpses. Through meditation, spiritual discipline, expanding consciousness, deep intimacy, our experience of the reality of this world can change to bring us closer to a state of bliss and unity. But for the lesser-evolved fish, the oceanic experience of unity is found through the avoidance of discipline and responsibility, and indulgence in escapism.

Alcohol and drug abuse is a shadow side of Pisces. But there are other, perhaps less insidious aspects to the shadow that can also be dangerous in large enough doses. Too much television, food, sex, sleep. Anything that brings pleasure, distraction from pain, and avoidance of responsibility can be used as a vehicle to escape.

Those Pisceans who use escape and avoidance as regular survival tactics can, needless to say, make unattractive bedmates. Self-indulgence that is born of passivity and lack of will has all the strength of a wet tissue, and can certainly be a turn-off. The real business of life—the responsibility of earning a living and keeping some sort of order, paying bills and ensuring that the basics of survival are taken care of—all falls to the partner. Passivity can be very charming in a childlike sort of way, and the intricacies of a soul-to-soul connection a heady and addictive delight, but without the balance of real-life awareness, everything falls apart. Saturn is symbolic of this need for order, boundaries, limitations, controls, discipline. Neptune, Pisces' ruler, is the opposite—being symbolic of the breaking down of boundaries, of dissolution and transcendence, or overcoming the limitations of physical life. When Pisces falls into the shadow, it is Neptune's dark side that reigns supreme in the psyche of the individual—and this is the fish being described here. This variety of fish needs to wake up to himself, or all of his relationships will come to the same unhappy conclusion.

The urge of Pisces to dissolve boundaries and merge, combined with its faith in a transcendent ideal, means there is a reluctance to acknowledge anything that is less than ideal in a partner. Pisces wants to merge completely with an idealized lover; and because of its reluctance to recognize anything that is not completely ideal, there is often an element of fantasy, imagination, and illusion or deception creeping in. The fish will make herself believe that all is perfect, all is bliss—and this is nowhere more dangerous than in the realm of relationships. These Pisceans can shackle themselves to fraudsters, losers, and wasters—becoming martyrs and victims of their own refusal to stop dreaming and face the truth. The rose-tinted glasses are a permanent fixture with these people, and it is this that accounts for the high number of Pisceans who end up as life's victims.

Another manifestation of this idealization can be seen in those Pisceans who break up their relationships because they fall short of the ideal. In their imaginations, love and romance are states of perfect bliss. The real-life version can never measure up, and so the Pisces has a feeling of not being loved enough. Elizabeth Taylor is an example of this. She is quoted as saying something along the lines of, "I always felt I could never be loved enough." That accounts, no doubt, for the number of marriages she entered into. The quest for the perfect, ideal, Neptunian, boundless love is a strong motivation for the deluded fish.

She drifts, all she wants to do with her life is lose it somewhere.
—Dorothy Baker

At the other end of that continuum from the victim, Pisces is known for its urge to "rescue" others (other victims). It is the intense empathy of Pisces, the compassion and sensitivity to others' wounds, that makes them particularly susceptible to sad stories. Too susceptible to bleeding hearts, Pisces is easily moved by appeals to her empathy. This is all fine, and of course Pisceans fulfill an important role in the world—hospice volunteers, workers in institutions where people are suffering from various physical and emotional wounds. But where this urge becomes dark is where personal and family relationships are neglected because of the needs of the collective. Because Neptune is about universal love, love that is boundless, personal love can be the second rung down for those fish who are unable to establish true intimacy. Everyone else's needs then become a substitute, and they are seen as more important than those nearest and dearest. These are the people who work as volunteers for telephone counseling services, but neglect their own children's or partner's emotional, and even physical, needs.

And then there is the merging of the two—victim and rescuer—in the codependent relationship. This is where the helper or rescuer reinforces the dependency of the sick person or victim. Piscean shadowlands are heavily populated with codependents. Self-destructive people easily ensnare gullible and compassionate Pisceans—and the dynamics are in place for codependency to develop. The Pisces woman married to the alcohol abuser is a classic example of this. She believes she loves this man, and that love means she has to save him from himself, that he needs her to survive. In reality, she needs him every bit as much as he needs her, because he feeds her urge to be the rescuer, or the martyr. She is a Pisces woman without clear boundaries, without a clear sense of herself, so she merges her identity with her partner, and his self-destructiveness drags them both down. Unless she recognizes what is happening, she can be destroyed in the process.

Pisces can also find herself drawn to abusive relationships, her compassion for her abuser keeping her locked into the relationship for far too many years. She is a true victim, and has come to this place through an inability to put boundaries in place that define her value: what she will accept and what she will not. She just keeps accepting. She is passive and yielding, to the point where her spirit is crushed out of existence.

The dark side of Pisces is not easily remedied. Awareness is our purpose here—and if the one you love is a Piscean creature who has fallen into the shadow side, then the best and most loving thing you can do is gently appraise him of a few "realities" of the world. That bottle of wine each night is not going to bring any lasting peace; avoiding pain by trying to escape from it, rather than facing it, keeps it alive.

Pisces hearts need to be heard before they can be healed of the grief that life pain has inflicted. Listen, support, give love, but don't rescue (that recipe for codependence); encouragement to find their inner strength is important. Their highest potential is boundless love, but it needs to be tempered with awareness of their own value and the need for boundaries. These gentle hearts need to know they are loved and supported, and they need to have their gifts acknowledged. With this, the light gradually overcomes the dark. Love does conquer all for this sign. If they don't get there this time around, it matters not—they have an eternity.

Compatibility

Pisces is most compatible with fellow water signs Scorpio and Cancer. However, this is a generalization—and the most important indicator of true compatibility is the picture that emerges from a blending of the two birth charts. The Sun is but one component of many. That being said, Pisces needs to feel emotional rapport, to feel the soul, in its relationships—and who can do that better than the other water signs?

Air is often attracted to Pisces and vice versa. This is about some serious learning, and the universe seems to arrange these things—not to bring us unending harmony, but to test us. As mentioned under Aquarius, there is an "unusual" harmony in the attraction of this sign with Pisces—despite the fact it is air, and theoretically not a good match. When air and water get together, there are always going to be some obstacles on the river.

Earth has an affinity with Pisces, but too much water can turn earth to mud—so the balance needs to be maintained. Earth can be too dry, too materially oriented, for dreamy Pisces. On the other hand, Pisces can bring to earth a slice of something otherworldly, and that can be both healing and soothing to the earth signs.

The fire signs are theoretically not the greatest with watery Pisces—but there can be a lot of steam generated in a positive way. All depends on the consciousness levels of the parties. And again, on other elements in their combined charts.

Relationship Clues

If you are in a relationship with a Pisces, the thing to be aware of is your partner's intense need to connect, soul to soul. You may wonder what this really means, but it is not as complex as it might sound. The soul is always giving clues to its needs. For Pisces, creating soft atmospheres with gentle music and lighting, looking deeply into the eyes (windows of the soul), holding, touching, connecting physically—these are a few of the ways the soul is moved. Essentially, anything that takes you both out of the mundane world and into the world of spirit will keep the magic alive in your relationship.

There is much Pisces can tolerate, if spirit is attended to. Long separations, lack of prioritization, things that other signs would see as reasons to quit can be transcended by the fish—who lives under a different set of rules anyway. But neglect the connection of the soul, and the relationship will slowly fade away. She may be there in body, but her soul will be seeking other refuges. Sadly, these may be found in escapist pastimes . . . so if you really love your girl or boy fish, then be there, not just in body but also in soul. Bring heart to your relationship in whatever ways you can. Small things count—and Pisces is ever alert to the small things. That edge to your voice, that impatience, small acts of neglect can, for the fish, be painfully wounding. Take responsibility in the practicalities of life—this is never the strong point of Pisces, particularly the women.

This relationship, if you can keep the soul present, will key you in to your own hidden depths, which is truly a gift. It is one that makes being fully conscious and awake to the ways of the soul in your union, and at the same time anchored firmly in the physical world, worth the effort it may take.

Your Higher Destiny

Life is not a problem to be solved,
but a mystery to be lived.
—Thomas Merton

To understand things we must have been once in them
and then come out of them;
so that first there must be captivity
and then deliverance,
illusion, followed by disillusion,
enthusiasm by disappointment.
He who is still under the spell,
and he who has never felt the spell,
are equally incompetent.
—Henri-Frédéric Amiel

We each have a higher ground beckoning us. Our higher destiny is to fulfill our soul's intention, our plan for this life. The Sun signs are the clues and keys to what our soul needs to vitalize the personality, and where we can best direct our energies, in the quest of individuation.

When we aim for the higher ground, we are on the way to fully becoming all we can be. Each sign has its strengths and its weaknesses, as we've seen. Eliminating the weakness inherent in our Sun sign is a matter of awareness and intention. In the following reflections, I have tried to illuminate the essence and higher potential of each sign—at times through pointing out its pitfalls. With this awareness, you can set the intention to make the most of the opportunity this life is giving you to heal and evolve.

Intention is powerful. But we are all human, and the human condition is necessarily a fractured one. We will not get it right all the time. Most of us are lifetimes away from sainthood.

That's why we're here. Learning, failing, growing, and learning some more are the name of the game, and all part of the mystery that is this life.

We shouldn't be afraid to make mistakes. And we may need to redefine the word *mistake*. When a movie is filmed, there are often a number of takes for each scene. Our lives are like a movie, and we are playing the lead role. Part of the plan is to make mistakes, because that's how we get it into heart and soul. *It* being the lesson we are working on at the time. Many of our lessons involve our relationships.

Relationship "failures" are usually failures only in our (or society's) limited understanding. On a soul level, a "failed marriage," for example, may be in fact the perfect outcome! We may have completed some important karma with that individual. The whole purpose of our coming together may have been to do exactly what we did, for the time we did. So on that level of awareness, there are no mistakes and there are no failures—as long as we learn from the experience. We all know people who keep creating the same old karma over and over again. It is hard to be consciously aware of your soul journey and stay stuck in the same pattern.

Looking at the opposite sign to our own can be a valuable exercise, as each of the signs operates in a binary oppositional pair. The opposite sign, then, contains within it the seeds we need to integrate, to more fully realize the purity of our own soul journey. For example, Aries' courage and self-assertiveness is lifted to the higher ground when it is infused with Libran awareness of others. Virgo's efficiency and eye for detail reaches a higher ground when it encompasses some of Pisces' awareness of the big picture.

Each sign is enlarged in consciousness when it strives to unite the polarities of its opposite sign.

Aries

The higher destiny of Aries is to infuse your actions with courage, through the energy of your spirit. You have a pure, fearless, knowing essence. This you must learn to trust. Your intuition is strong, but you are usually so immersed in the activities and challenges of life that you do not always hear it. If you can still yourself on a daily basis and tune inward, you will come to know that voice—call it intuition, the soul, or your higher self. Then take that knowingness and, trusting it, energize all you do with it. You will arouse others from their habitual mindset of dependence on the false securities of the ego. You will startle them out of their complacency when they see you acting with complete faith and the thrill and exuberance of entering fully into all life offers—embracing all, the highs and the lows.

With your natural courage and assertiveness, you are a born leader. The quality of your leadership needs to be imbued with soul ahead of ego. So often with you the ego dominates—because Aries' primary motive is physical survival, which is the domain of the ego. The ego's role is to ensure we know we are separate (it fools us well) so we take care of ourselves and survive in these bodies.

It is very easy, therefore, for you to run with the ego and shut out the voice of your soul. Deepening your connection to the Infinite is the task your higher destiny is asking of you. You need to become more aware of your connections with others—seeing them less as threats to your own survival, less as competition, and more as souls who could do with some help from your courage and insight.

With your ability to lead and your willingness to engage in life, you are perfectly equipped to encourage and inspire those less able. It doesn't mean you become a charity worker. Rather, the point is, in becoming more conscious of others' needs, you deepen your awareness of the One, the connection we all share; this will soothe and still the voice of your ego.

Others are not a threat to you; they are playing the same game. Together you can help each other. In these times, we do not have to fight to survive. We must learn, rather, to surrender the idea of separateness and embrace our connections to those with whom we are sharing the planet. Good leaders carry this responsibility and this awareness—and this is your destiny.

You are: strong, courageous, intuitive, passionate, feisty, energetic, impulsive, willful.

You can learn from your opposite sign: Libra can teach you to cooperate with others rather than put yourself and your own needs at the head of the list. Learn to listen more to what your partner is saying. Hear his perspective, his truth. You can attract more flies with honey—so take a leaf from Libra's book and aim to please others first. Train yourself to be the witness. Watch yourself in action, in speech. Then you will become aware of the positives of inaction, of standing still. There is a time for action and a time to cease from acting. Libra has awareness of the value of waiting, considering, pausing, and deliberating. You can infuse your self-directed power with this awareness, and your actions will become even more potent.

Some of your symbols in the outer world are: the planet Mars, sporting competitions (as participant or spectator), heroic journeys, acts of bravery, winning, trailblazing (pioneering), the color red, the number 1, iron, diamonds, the head, spicy food (mustard, chilies), capers, sheep, and knives. England, France, and Germany are Aries countries; Naples, Florence, and Marseilles are Aries cities.

Your body and spirit need you to: use your vast reservoirs of energy in physically challenging sports and exercise; tune in to the spirit of nature, absorbing the vitality of the Sun by walking, running, biking in clean open spaces; strengthen your body through disciplining your mind; soften, hold on to your thoughts before sending them out in wounding arrows; find inner peace through looking for the deeper meaning of your outer journeys.

Your soul needs you to: relax your fight. Listen to your intuition, loosen your grip, and trust in higher powers to ensure your survival. You cannot *not* survive. You are an eternal being, and your consciousness will go on after you leave this life. You are also part of a bigger whole, and it will serve you to have the cooperation of others. You do this by putting aside your own desires, at times, to listen to their needs. Your consciousness and the quality of your life depends on your realization that there is strength in numbers—and you are the one most equipped to be leader! Use your physicality well by infusing it with the strength of your spirit. Together, they make an awesomely powerful team—strong but soft, daring but steady: the enthusiasm, energy, and spontaneity of a child combined with the wisdom and sensitivity to others of an integrated adult. This, Aries, is your promise and your potential.

Taurus

Your higher destiny is to liberate yourself from the attachment to any concerns for physical survival, and feel the deep serenity and peace that comes from immersing yourself in the natural world. You illuminate yourself and others by understanding the true nature of desire—that which flows in perfect accord with natural law.

You have a deep affinity with the desires of the natural, physical world, and this ultimately needs to be understood as a complete trust in the world of desire to lead you back to spirit. Free yourself from the bonds of possessiveness and materialism—these are simply a means to an end. Transmuting your need for security and the desire to feel the reassuring presence of material comforts and physical pleasures into artistic and creative expression is your higher destiny.

As you free yourself from the chains that bind you to the world of the physical, you open up new vistas that allow you to express your instinctive appreciation for the beauty and texture of physical existence. As you allow yourself to join with the creative energy of the universe, you silence the voice of the security-driven ego and bring the beauty and strength of your aesthetic awareness into material form. You discover, then, that you are safe, you have always been safe, and you will always be safe—because you are being nurtured by the hand that brought you here. That same hand will take you away again, and all your fighting to insulate yourself from the inevitability of this ultimate loss will be for naught. It could happen at any time.

Your higher destiny is to discover that all your creations in the world of form are intended to be carriers and expressions of the Infinite. They have no permanence, and this is your grand discovery—there is no permanence, but you can have peace! Your avenue to this discovery runs through natural law and the quiet presence and serenity you feel when you open yourself to it.

Only in the formless will you ultimately learn there is permanence. Your persistence and insistence that life keep you safe will be seen for the illusion it is when you open your eyes and your heart to the reality that only in the serenity of the natural world will you find the security you seek. Your desires in the physical world *are* ultimately spiritual ones.

The world is an illusion, albeit a persistent one. The world of form is the illusion, but it is an illusion capable of leading to the truth—if you follow the dictates of natural law. It is right to honor the physical world, the impermanent world of form, because it is simply the visible side of the whole. Your mission is to know this for the truth it is, and then to use your Taurean gift, your affinity with form and with the earth, to demonstrate to others the serenity that comes with this knowing.

Fears and insecurities, and doubts in the intrinsic value of the world of form, are the currency of the ego and need to be seen by you for what they are. Your path to serenity is the slow and sure one of walking on the earth—as an enlightened soul who knows how to play in form; you become the alchemist, transmuting the lead of solid matter into the gold of sacred artistic expression. It is your higher destiny to create, in form, works revealing—to the eye that truly sees—the beauty of the invisible, which lies behind the visible.

You are: tenacious, enduring, resolute, creative, inspirational, sensuous, reliable.

You can learn from your opposite sign: Scorpio can teach you to go beneath the surface, to think about the nature of power and the origin of everything on the visible level. Scorpio knows the secret: the world of form is the effect, not the cause. Learn to go to the source. The body becomes sick after the psyche (soul) has first become imbalanced. The beautiful painting originates in the soul of the artist. Scorpio knows about the power of the invisible. You can bring this knowledge to your creativity. Learn from Scorpio, too, the value of letting go, releasing, what you no longer need. Know when to stop holding on. Cease resisting the ebb and flow of life's current. Nothing lasts forever, all is in a state of flux. Change is the only constant.

Some of your symbols in the outer world are: the planet Venus, comfort food, cereals, creative arts and crafts, pottery, poppies, daisies, foxglove, emeralds, the throat and thyroid gland, interior decor, cloves, spearmint, cattle, and the colors pink, pale blue, and green. Ireland, Switzerland, and Iran are Taurus countries; Dublin and St. Louis are Taurus cities.

Your body and spirit need you to: spend time in nature by gardening, touching the earth, planting; use your hands to create with clay, wood, fabric, paint; massage, soothe, and shift energy with your hands; create objects of beauty; enjoy the feel of the wind on your face; move your body and feel it as an extension of your spirit.

Your soul needs you to: relax your grip on the material world. Trust in the ebbs and flows of life. There is a plan for your life, and you do not need to obsess over the outer world to the exclusion of the inner. Your strengths are your innate feel for the beauty of the physical world and your ability to bring this into the world of form through your creative expression. You illuminate and inspire others when you trust in life and open yourself to the flow and wherever it may take you, creating as you go spaces and objects of beauty. Be aware always that the more you hold on to the world of form, the less room there is for spirit to play in your life. In letting go of possessions, you make space for the only possessions that matter, those of the soul, to enter in. This is your promise and your potential.

——————————— *Gemini* ———————————

Your higher destiny is to experience wonder in the interconnecting world of ideas. Your journey is one of endless learning. You need to be continually surprised, endlessly curious about life and all its wonders. Communicating the relevance and value of change and generalization (as opposed to specialization) by embracing these in your own life inspires others. Making connections with others through opening your heart and your mind and demonstrating willingness to change outer reality is what destiny requires of you.

In the ego-dominated minds of many, change is threatening and highly resisted. The cost of holding on to the known, whether it be old and unconscious thought patterns or situations in the outer life (one being a reflection of the other), is the retreat of soul consciousness. And the price one pays for the retreat of the soul is alienation from the Infinite. It is deadening to your spirit to stay in comfortable ruts, or to stick to the tried and true path. The soul is only encountered in the freshness of the new—relinquishing old habits, learning new skills—and it is your higher destiny to awaken others to this reality.

Your willingness and your desire to pursue new learning, new pastures, and new experiences opens you to the vastness of thought forms on offer in this world. This is not a lifetime for specialization, and you must learn to cut the shackles of mental limitation.

You have the quickness and agility of mind to sense the possibilities of the new, but your Achilles' heel can be your fear of losing what you have in the process. You need to trust your ability to adjust, to adapt to the flux of life and to connect and relate with others; you have all you need for this journey. This is your higher potential—to make connections with others through your multi-faceted interests. You then become an inspiration and a potent source of learning for others.

Your natural fickleness and restlessness sometimes need curbing so you can find the time to give significance to your discoveries. It is breadth and depth that will lead you to the relationships your soul craves. Skimming too fast over the surface sabotages the freedoms you gain by your endless learning. Breadth, through openness to change and depth, through stilling the mind and opening the heart, is the key. You have the capacity with your dual nature to do both—and this is your task. Covering the ground is not sufficient in itself—you must be aware of what you are here for and where your learning is taking you. The ants, too, remember, are busy. It is what you are busy *about* that counts.

You are: agile, quick, adaptable, changeable, communicative, a bridge builder.

You can learn from your opposite sign: Sagittarius can teach you to find meaning in your knowledge. Slow down your quest to acquire new knowledge sufficiently that you have the time to go deeper, and then you will discover the higher meaning behind the outer form. Learn a language so you can see inside the culture, the minds of the people. Slow down and look for the symbols, the signs. Look for the essence within the form. Seek out truth. Listen to others' truth. In conversation, challenge yourself to listen with greater depth. Train yourself to keep your mind open and still, without formulating an immediate response. Your mind is quick, but it needs disciplining. From that open, still space, Sagittarian insights will emerge. Your life will take on greater meaning and greater depth.

Some of your symbols in the outer world are: the planet Mercury, talking, computers, telephones, pairs of anything, letters, books, lavender, lily-of-the-valley, ferns, agate, nuts, the nervous system, talking birds, monkeys, butterflies, bridges, the shoulders, arms, hands, and the colors light yellow and brights. Wales, Belgium, and Egypt are Gemini places; London, San Francisco, and Melbourne are Gemini cities.

Your body and spirit need you to: move lightly through life, dance, play, keep moving, discuss, share your thoughts, acquire knowledge, and find time to be still each day and quiet your mind, dream, meditate. Keep your thoughts to yourself—allowing them to grow and mature into wisdom.

Your soul needs you to: believe in the true purpose of your constant journeying. You are here to create connections with others, to understand relationships, to be an example of fluidity, adaptability, and openness to the new as avenues for the soul to enter into life. In relinquishing security fears and trusting the truism that whenever one door closes another opens, you become an inspiration for others. Your gift is your ability to let go and start again—but you need to do so without looking back, without worrying about where the road you are on is taking you. Making connections with others, building bridges, being the communicator—these are your strengths. The higher destiny of "the messenger" that you are is to spark with a childlike eagerness and enthusiasm in discovering the new, and then to steady yourself for long enough to understand its significance. Infuse your relationships with the vitality and energy of the new. In this way you become truly inspirational and your partnerships thrive. This is your promise and your potential.

Cancer

Your higher destiny is to find your place in the world, your sense of belonging, by opening your heart to the universal consciousness. Neptune, your esoteric ruler, symbolizes the transcendent realm— so you have an innate feeling for the unity of life, which lies beyond your individual consciousness. Because of your intense sensitivity, which you are afraid to allow yourself to feel at times, you can close yourself off from the source of strength and support of the universal consciousness that would be open to you.

If you can shut down the frightened voice of the ego that has you believing you are a helpless child alone in the universe, and trust in your connection with the divine, you can love more fully, more universally. All of humanity will benefit from a love like yours. Your instinctive nurturing becomes free to care for all without conditions and dependencies. When the illusion of separation falls away, you lose your tenacious grip, your desperate hold on the people and situations you feel you need in order to belong. You trust instead that you belong already, that you are a child of the universe. You then become a nurturer of many, extending your great capacity to love and care beyond your immediate circle.

The world needs your generosity of heart, your sensitivity and attunement to the emotional cues of others, when, and only when, they have extended beyond the infantile needs of the self. It is only when you go beyond the reaches of your immediate circle and allow the soul to enter in that you can love with all the largeness of spirit you have within you.

Your destiny is to be a caregiver in the largest sense of the word. You allow the soul to enter in when you can disarm your history, become conscious of the origin of your habit patterns, and live from a place of trust in the process of life. This is your higher destiny.

You are: caring, compassionate, sensitive, defensive, protective, open to intangibles.

You can learn from your opposite sign: Capricorn can teach you to discipline your moods so you are not held sway by them. There are times when emotional detachment is helpful, but do not be afraid to feel your feelings. Learn to put your best foot forward, even on those days when you are in the swamplands of negative emotions. When you detach from your too-feeling nature, knowing, as Capricorn does, that "this too shall pass," you can access a higher awareness, universal consciousness. With greater detachment from your feelings, confusion will ease and the path will become clearer. Remember that your feelings are not real; they are waves of energy, that is all. Focus more on the material plane, as Capricorn readily does, when you feel overwhelmed.

Some of your symbols in the outer world are: the Moon, pregnancy, motherhood, boats, milk, photography, cameras, antiques, the chest and breasts, pearls, crabs, turtles, family trees, white flowers, roses, lilies, and the colors silver, smoky gray, cream, and pearlescent. Scotland, Holland, the USA, and northern Africa are Cancer places; Amsterdam, Stockholm, Milan, Venice, New York, and Tokyo are Cancer cities.

Your body and spirit need you to: cleanse your auric field with the healing power of water, swim, bathe, shower, spend time by the sea, sit outside on a full Moon and soak in her light, hold stones and gems of the earth and feel your connection with other forms of consciousness, cook nourishing food for your family and friends, learn about your ancestors and study the patterns of your genetic inheritance.

Your soul needs you to: relinquish your old defenses. Realize they are the workings of the insecure child—and no longer relevant to your life in the new consciousness. Trust in your inner knowing. You feel, acutely, the pains and emotions of life—and your task is to clarify whether these are helpful or not. They are helpful if they strengthen your connections with others and your awareness and compassion for the human condition. They are not helpful if they become an invitation to retreat, to enter into your own inner defensive space. Know that your mission here is bigger than that. Your gift of feeling is both your curse and your blessing, but only you can choose which of those you will act out in the world. That choice hinges on the power of your belief in your constant companion, your higher self. Always present, you are in fact always at home in the world. You are not here to seek mothering, but to be the mother—you have the heart for it and the compassion and sensitivity for it, and this is your promise and your potential.

Leo

Your higher destiny is to use your creativity and joyful self-expression as a channel for the divine. You are gifted with a capacity to manifest in the three-dimensional world, but you need to become aware of the higher imperative of your talents: that is, they must be used to lighten the path for others. The ego is the dragon you must slay—as it is even more powerful in you than the other signs.

You have been compensated with a large measure of creative ability and a lightness of heart. You are learning how to trust and how to enjoy your life, and you have all you need for this journey. You come from the heart, but your learning centers around knowing your heart beats not just within you but within the Mind of God. Your creative expressions need to be examples of the light within you and shared freely. Every talent we possess has been lent to us; it is not ours, but ours to use in sharing it with others.

You are a natural ruler, but you may need to understand that true rulers have first and foremost rulership over their own lower natures. You are destined to stand tall, as the bright, joyous, light-filled creature that you are—and to do so, you need to be unimpeded by the pulls of the ego to be acknowledged, praised, respected, admired. When these things matter less to you than the knowledge within your own heart, that you are being true to yourself and you are giving your gifts for the sake of giving, they will come to you without being sought.

Create for the joy it brings to others, and not solely for the admiration that comes to you from your talents. There are many things you can do in the world as the ruler you are—but to truly rule, you must be in touch with your soul first. This is your higher destiny, Leo.

You are: generous, creative, warm-hearted, impressive, powerful, joyous, talented, forgiving.

You can learn from your opposite sign: Aquarius can teach you to let go of the ego-driven desire to stand out and, instead, take your place as one of humanity—one, it is true, in possession of a natural nobility. Allow your heart light to shine unimpeded by the ego's childlike demand to be noticed. Aquarius knows we all matter; no one is ultimately more important than another. This awareness would benefit you. Your big heart is a tremendous gift to others, but it needs to come from a pure space. Aquarius can teach you to look to the future, to move with the changing times that are taking us all to a less ego-centered, more heart-ruled existence.

Some of your symbols in the outer world are: the Sun, royalty, performance sports, theatre, flamboyant costumes, sunflowers, marigolds, honey, saffron, the heart and spine, gold, rubies, the cat family, palm trees, citrus, and the colors gold, orange, and golden yellow. Italy, Romania, the Czech Republic, and Iraq are Leo countries; Rome, Philadelphia, Los Angeles, Mumbai, and Chicago are Leo cities.

Your body and spirit need you to: recharge with the rays of the Sun; sunbathe; walk on the beach; keep your spine supple and strong with exercise, sports, and yoga; laugh; have fun with your children; create; be romantic; organize and coordinate social activities.

Your soul needs you to: release your attachment to the ego's demands and believe in your own power. Yours is the path of a leader of the heart, and your call is to be bigger in spirit. As you relinquish the desire to be praised and acknowledged, you refuse the ego and gain greater control over your thoughts and emotions. Rest in the knowledge that your gifts of creativity, insight, and joy in the process of life are the roads you may take to your higher self. You have been given the path of pleasure in manifesting on the material plane, and that is something to be truly grateful for. Give thanks regularly for your life and use the blessings of your open heart and generous spirit to amplify the experience of life for others. Your creations will then open others' hearts and rebound back to you as a deeper, more meaningful experience of your own life's journey. This is your promise and your potential.

Virgo

Your higher destiny is to attain clarity on the nature of matter, the source of it—spirit—and where you fit in. Matter and spirit are one and the same; the difference is only in the level of density—matter having the greater density. Thus, the physical body and the spiritual body are two aspects of the same whole. Your destiny is to humbly honor both.

Your powers of discrimination have been given to you to be used in service to humanity. Until you know that you and others are part of the one whole, your discerning eye may fall into the error of separatist thinking—the belief that you are here to fix things, make them more perfect, because others are unable to. Your nervousness is symptomatic of the unease of erroneous thinking—your critical tendencies, likewise. You are not here to make things more perfect, or to make others do your bidding, but rather to give of yourself for the sake of giving.

Service is your path to your higher destiny, and although it may sound less than the glamorous life you would envisage for yourself, it is in actuality the right path for you. You turn away from it, and you neglect your soul's intentions.

The ego would have you believe that a more perfect life is your divine right and urge you to step over others to get there. Your challenge is to silence mental noise and embrace your true role as, first, a giver of service to others.

The Moon is your esoteric ruler, and as with Cancer, the sign whose natural ruler is the Moon, your role is to care and nurture. As you apply your abilities for soothing, calming, and healing, you will come to know true humility, your higher destiny. Peace of mind and heart is there, just around the corner from the harried quest for perfection. It is there in the silence of unconditional regard and compassion for others and unselfish service. This is your higher calling and your path to freedom.

You are: meticulous, fussy, practical, diligent, perfection-seeking, analytical, modest.

You can learn from your opposite sign: Pisces can teach you to see the bigger picture. You lose yourself in the detail, and this affects your nervous system. Relax, release, and go with the flow as Pisces does. Try to see the impact of your actions on others. We are all weavers of the one web. Pisces feels, innately, the universality of life. Learn from Pisces how to open to the moment and loosen your grip on life; let go of the need to control, let go of the fear, and trust in the compassionate nature of life to support you. Give yourself unstintingly to help and support others.

Some of your symbols in the outer world are: the planet Mercury, detailed patterns, mentoring, hygiene, fine handcrafts, small flowers (buttercups, forget-me-nots), root vegetables, the stomach and intestines, mercury and nickel, sardonyx, diet, massage, and the colors navy blue and green. Brazil, Turkey, and Greece are Virgo countries; Paris and Athens are Virgo cities.

Your body and spirit need you to: garden; plant; allow the earth to absorb your nervous energy; spend time in the countryside; stroke your cat; do craft work; care for children, animals, the sick, and dependent; give your energy selflessly; sit quietly and still, body and mind, in meditation; nurture your body with natural foods and calm your spirit with gentle exercise.

Your soul needs you to: understand that you are here to give value to the universe through service to others. You have an innate ability to care for and connect with others, and you may turn away from this in your quest to create a more perfect life for yourself. You sometimes see only the holes in life and it feels too much. You need to see the whole, not the holes. This is your challenge, and you have been given the gift of discernment to help beam you to the places, people, and situations that are most in need of your selflessness. First you need to slay that dragon of selfishness in your own heart. Preoccupation with the self comes from an awareness of imperfection, so the motive may be pure, but it is doing you no good and no good is being contributed to the world. Accept that the world is imperfect, as we all are—and make your quest that of offering your gifts where you can. As you do, you will be given more than you could ever have had by taking any other path. This is your promise and your potential.

Libra

Your higher destiny is to learn the secret of right human relations through finding the equilibrium point between the polarities of life. This midpoint is your key to the peace your soul craves: perfect balance through a tolerance for paradox. Learning to be decisive, ironically, is part of the journey toward achieving this tolerance.

Your esoteric ruler is Uranus—ruler of the higher mind. You have the ability to tune in to a more advanced level of intuition and to use this to make the right choice, the one aligned with the highest good. Your tendency to sit on the fence, because you see "both sides" and dislike the idea of choosing one over the other, will transform as you evolve with the power of spiritual insight. Trust this connection you have.

In perfect balance, nothing happens. We are here to *do* in this physical life, which means we have to decide to act. There is no such thing as a wrong decision, and therefore you need not be afraid of making the wrong one. Instead, trust in the knowledge that you are guided by a higher voice than your own, and the very act of making a decision will give you strength of character and stabilize your life's journey—in a way your equivocating would never do.

Understanding the secret of right relations is then a matter of putting aside self-interest and asking the universe the question: what decision needs to be made here? Go within, where the answers will always be. But first, quiet the voice of the ego—the voice that would have you believe you need to have it all, and to commit yourself to one direction would eliminate such possibility. Commit you must if you are to fulfill your higher destiny. Strength and certainty (paradoxically) will be yours when you do, because of your innate understanding of justice. You will gain in all ways when you trust your inner knowing. And in this way you will draw others to you for guidance and insight. You will be respected as the mediator and ambassador of the heart you then will be.

You are: charming, easygoing, diplomatic, indecisive, flirtatious, peaceable.

You can learn from your opposite sign: Aries can teach you to be more assertive, to seize the day and act. Your equivocation, your reluctance to choose, so often wastes your time and energy. Take a cue from Aries and be more conscious of acting on your own behalf. You will find that when you do, events miraculously unfold and things begin to move in your life—rather than exist in a state of immobilized homeostasis. Aries has courage, and this is a quality you can draw from your opposite sign. Against a backdrop of death, what is so terrifying? Fear not the judgments or opinions of others. Stand strong and firm in your thoughts and be decisive in your actions. Aries energy will bring much forward movement to your life.

Some of your symbols in the outer world are: the planet Venus, scales, diplomats, meditation, relationships, the kidneys, roses, blue flowers, raspberries, strawberries, apples, pears, jade, sapphires, reptiles, and the colors pink, blue, and pale green. Austria, Canada, Tibet, Japan, and Argentina are Libra countries; Copenhagen, Frankfurt, and Vienna are Libra cities.

Your body and spirit need you to: keep the air moving in your lungs with activity and exercise; make one positive, spontaneous choice every day; learn to say no; create an environment that is calming, harmonious, free from clutter, and make that your refuge; leave your work at work and create a home that is your sanctuary. You need inner tranquility and a balance between action and nonaction.

Your soul needs you to: create serenity and harmony both on an outer level and an inner one. As you open up to the possibility of making active choices and living with the consequences, you gain strength of character, which, almost ironically, leads to greater internal peace. Peace is your soul's greatest desire. The most successful people in a material sense make decisions quickly. Those who have inner peace also make decisions affirmatively. Life cannot be free from conflict and disharmony all the time, and you need to make more active choices to avoid the inner dissonance your indecisiveness creates. Life is not a popularity contest, and we are all urged to make choices—these choices become statements about who we are, what our values are, what we stand for, and what we do not. Remember: in perfect balance, nothing happens. Understanding the nature of relationships, that balance point between the polarities, means aligning yourself with your intuitive, higher self and finding where you stand, making judgment calls in order to know yourself. This is the ultimate reason you need to choose—choosing defines who you really are, for yourself and for others. This is your promise and your potential.

—————————— *Scorpio* ——————————

Your higher destiny is to transform the desires of your l
ture into the aims of the soul through making the unc
conscious. Yours is a difficult path in many ways, but it is one that
carries great reward. You have the capacity to heal and transform
others, when you have put your own demons to rest. This mission,
if you choose to accept it, will open you up to the power centers in
the universe, and your personal power will be greatly amplified.

This lifetime for you is about refining your soul, ridding yourself of the dross of dark karma and old wounding from the past.
Because karma has an attracting energy, you can be drawn to the
dark elements of life—and herein lies your greatest challenge.

With the planet Mars as your esoteric ruler, you have a fierce
individualized energy, and this can be used to determine your
higher pathway. It is about getting past the pull of personality for
you. The people you choose to have around you are vital. Stronger
personalities can lure you into the dark side. You need to determine your own path, set your own goals.

Understand that you have a deep and intense feeling nature—
and this is your blessing, in fact. You are here to know the depths, so
you can help others to understand the world of the invisible and be
transformed by this knowledge. Use your energy to go to the root and
see what really motivates people, and use your emotional awareness to
create a career and a life path that supports your own emotional well-
being and that of those around you. This is your higher destiny.

You are: passionate, determined, emotional, powerful, obsessive,
    secretive.

You can learn from your opposite sign: Taurus can teach you to be
    anchored in the here and now, in the natural world of physi-
    cal, tangible reality. Sometimes your probing and penetrating
    of the hidden motives and agendas of others becomes too over-
    whelming. Take a cue from Taurus and occupy yourself with

material reality on a regular basis. Spend time in nature and in the uncomplicated body; forget the mind and its secrets. Carve out regular time to just be, without awareness of anything other than the preciousness of the moment. This will bring you back down to earth.

Some of your symbols in the outer world are: the planet Pluto, research, nocturnal creatures, espionage, birth, death, the reproductive system, surgery, plumbing, opals, steel, scorpions, insects, rhododendrons, geraniums, dark red flowers, the colors deep red, maroon, black, and black-and-white stripes. Morocco, Norway, and Syria are Scorpio countries; New Orleans, Washington DC, Wellington, and Valencia are Scorpio cities.

Your body and spirit need you to: use the therapeutic power of water—swim, bathe, walk by the ocean, rivers, and lakes; meditate in the hours of darkness; learn about and respect the inner workings of the body; trust your innate healing powers, and use your power to enhance the lives of others; transform your emotions into healing action. Use water, instead of wine, to soothe your spirits when life pain grips you.

Your soul needs you to: make your quest one of the soul, not only the body. Healing of body and soul for you means learning your lessons. Go to the dark places and come back, not beaten but strengthened by what you've seen and felt. Yours, for a part of your life at least, is a journey to the depths, the psychological oceans of the unconscious, and the intent is to annihilate your own darkness, heal your wounds, and come back whole. As you integrate your own desires, you become the healer you are destined to be. Healing may be found in the example of your life. Choosing to live a life of freedom, not buying into the prevalent culture of fear, following a different path—this is healing for others. Through you, they discover that we all have the power to choose our own lives. Your intensity of emotion and feeling is destined to empower you—as long as you use it rightly. It can be a tightrope you walk, but your higher destiny is to take this path and become more fully the powerful individual you are. This is your promise and your potential.

Sagittarius

Your higher destiny is to make your life a spiritual quest that encompasses others, as well as yourself. You have an enormous breadth of vision; your life is lived in broad brushstrokes on a large canvas. You have journeyed far, and now, in this lifetime, your mission is to create a life that is in alignment with more spiritual goals, by attaching meaning to your experiences.

Goals that transcend personal self-interest and include one's fellow travelers are those of the higher-minded Sagittarius. Your expansiveness needs to be matched with a sense of purpose, or it becomes a fruitless search for meaning, and a lonely one. Life must be a lived experience; and knowledge, or even wisdom, without the backing of experience, is hollow.

But searching for meaning is not an end in itself. You must take your vision and apply it to a worthy goal. And *worthy* means a goal with the higher good of others at heart. Squander yourself for a purpose. Apply your wisdom to teaching others—sharing the insights, beliefs, and truths you have stumbled upon. To use these for selfish, egoic gain is truly not worthy of the gift you have been given.

Freedom, as the song goes, is just another word for nothing left to lose. Freedom is the driving force of your vision quest. Your urge to be free, to explore, to learn, to travel, and to expand your being in all directions needs to be anchored to a purpose that is more altruistic than self-centered, or you could end up with nothing left to lose. The danger for you is that in pursuing freedom and the desire to have more, you risk losing the people and the things that should matter most to you. The heart and the connections you have with others are to be prized above all else, and these need to be part of your vision quest, part of the goals that you are shooting for. If you are reckless with others, you may find out that freedom is a lonely place to be.

True, you will have learned much on the way. You may be wise and knowledgeable, but your heart will ache for the simple pleasures of intimacy and connection shared with loved ones, your fellow travelers. The road you are traveling on is not intended to be a narrow one, but a companionable one. You have the wisdom and the drive to travel far in this life, and to make great evolutionary strides in understanding the meaning of life. Just know that everything you do affects those in your circle and beyond. Be careful with their souls, and you will achieve the status of guru—if you choose. This is your promise and your potential.

You are: freedom-loving, optimistic, enthusiastic, generous, honest, philosophical.

You can learn from your opposite sign: Gemini can teach you to engage with others, to make connections, to bridge the gaps between people. The path of the wanderer is a lonely one if relationships are not honored. Gemini can teach you, too, to travel lightly, to cover more ground by releasing the need to judge and moralize. Everyone is on their own path, and judging them for where they are on the path is futile. When the search for meaning threatens to derail you, become more like Gemini and stay on the surface: talk to people, learn something new, read a novel. There is a place for superficiality, and Gemini can show you the value of that place.

Some of your symbols in the outer world are: the planet Jupiter, archery, foreign travel, horizons, philosophy, higher education, universities, horses, deer, topaz, blueberries, cinnamon, garlic, carnations, pink flowers, the hips, the thighs, the liver, and the colors purple and dark blue. Spain, Australia, and South Africa are Sagittarius countries; Toronto, Toledo (in Spain), and Avignon are Sagittarius cities.

Your body and spirit need you to: explore the world; learn; teach; travel; be adventurous; go horseback riding, kayaking, skydiving, and surfing; camp in the wilderness; pass on your life's wisdom to your children and others; be balanced and moderate in your diet; practice what you preach, and preach less.

Your soul needs you to: take responsibility not only for your own quest for freedom, but also for the well-being of those around you. Your esoteric ruler is the earth. Your flights of freedom need to be grounded, or they may turn in on themselves and become destructive. If there is no higher goal, no humanistic aim, behind your urge to expand your being, you can find yourself at the end of a road to nowhere, wondering what the journey was really all about. Your soul needs you to keep in mind that you have a responsibility here, to the other people in your life—and those beyond your immediate circle. In pursuing your aims to be free to live the way you want to, are you really being honest with yourself? The soul fragments in the face of self-dishonesty. Are your aims really more important than everyone else's? And have they, so far, brought you to a place of peace? The true aim, the mission you are on, is to make your life a vision quest that encompasses the needs of others and relinquishes negative judgments. Your adventurous spirit will then take you on soul journeys that open your heart to the true meaning of this earthly sojourn. This is your promise and your potential.

Capricorn

Your higher destiny is to break free of attachment to material forms and control as you journey toward integrity. Integrity means wholeness—of body, mind, and heart. You can be too authoritarian and controlling, especially with those close to you. The feeling you need to control things around you has, at its root, fear. Your mission is to release your fears around chaos, obscurity, poverty, and survival, and learn to trust.

Your ruler Saturn is symbolic of structures and controls, necessary in the physical world of form. However, Saturn is also associated with anxiety around survival and protecting your "forms" in the material world. This is ego confusing the purity and purpose of form. The challenge is a tough one—to silence the voice of ego and listen to the voice of your soul—and it may be met most effectively in the second half of life.

In the first part of life, you will be about reinforcing those structures, advancing your ambitions and achieving in the world. Later, when you reflect on the relationships you have and reflect on the meaning behind the drive to succeed, you will come to see that much of what you have deemed vital to your survival was, in fact, not necessary at all. Everything in the world of form is impermanent. And the only true security is to be found within. This is the truth your journey is taking you toward. Love is the healing force that will break down the barriers you erect between yourself and others. Don't discover this too late. Yes, achieving in the world is spiritual—if you are using your gifts well. It becomes anti-spirit if it becomes the sole driving force and if your success matters more to you than the people around you do. It is never okay to walk over others on the way to the top, not for a Capricorn soul, because your journey is that of integrity.

To use your clear abilities, determination, and resilience to overcome obstacles, to exercise discipline and self-restraint, to know the meaning of patience and at the same time to do what it takes to create your great work: these are the tools you have come in with for your journey. This is the right road for you on a personal level, but marrying all of this to a higher-minded awareness of your heart connections with others, and reaching out a helping hand to them, is the best karmic plan. Achieving for yourself and others at the same time—and thereby learning the true meaning of success—this is your higher destiny.

You are: practical, disciplined, ambitious, patient, careful, determined, humorous.

You can learn from your opposite sign: Cancer can teach you to soften your heart and feel your feelings, to listen to them and come more from the spaciousness of an open heart. Your drive to succeed, to climb to the top of the mountain, needs to be tempered with sensitivity—toward yourself as much as others. That harsh taskmaster within shouldn't be given so much power. Silence the superego and focus on gentleness. No one is judging you but yourself. Achievement is noble, but consider always the daily price it extracts. You need to be more consciously selfish, softer, as Cancer is. Be kinder to yourself, and more gentle to your loved ones.

Some of your symbols in the outer world are: the planet Saturn, lead, the skeleton, skin, bones, teeth, the knees, clock time, the law, institutions of power and authority, amethysts, pansies, pine and poplar trees, comfreys, the dark colors, gray, black, and brown. India, Mexico, and Afghanistan are Capricorn places; Oxford, Delhi, and Mexico City are Capricorn cities.

Your body and spirit need you to: go tramping, climbing, hiking, get into the outdoors, lie on your back on the earth, look at the sky and think about the planet spinning through space—and what you are doing on it, drop your reluctance to engage with others, look eye to eye and speak from the heart.

Your soul needs you to: remember that being on the top of the heap is worthy, but it is all the more worthy when you have the love, admiration, and respect of those dear to you close by. Your soul needs you to feels its presence as you go about your way in the world. You tend to neglect your soul needs in your ambitious drive to succeed, and then wonder why you end up the lone wolf. Keep your connections with others alive by paying attention to interpersonal skills. These are as important as learning the skills of your trade or profession. Everything we do in this life is returned to us in some time and place—this is natural law. If we break human-made laws, we are punished. Likewise, if we break universal laws, we experience the consequences in the form of our karma, and we suffer. The challenge your soul is urging you to accept is to embrace universal law as instinctively as you embrace human-made laws. That is, understand the importance of "as you sow, so shall you reap." Give unstintingly your time, your skills, but most of all the love you keep locked up in your heart—and you will receive back in kind. This is your promise and your potential.

Aquarius

Your higher destiny is to distribute your love and wisdom to humanity, and to use your gifts to advance the evolution of society. You are prone to distance yourself from others because you feel you are somehow "different." Don't let your natural detachment keep you from offering your gifts, which are sorely needed in these ego-driven times.

You have an intuitive understanding of the deeper meaning of the human condition and an unconditional regard for all people, from all walks of life. Your ability to detach your ego is a wonderful attribute when it comes to helping others. Lesser emotions like jealousy and greed are not part of the make-up of the higher Aquarius. You have an innate willingness to share the power; your ego doesn't require applause and admiration. You help because you know we are all in this together, and you will do what you can.

A less-evolved Aquarius may use detachment as a way of avoiding interpersonal commitments—and therefore his gifts are inaccessible. This water bearer is misguidedly selfish, or more accurately, she is unconscious. This is not what you are here for. You are here to use your far-seeing awareness for the good of the whole. Using the energies of Uranus, planet of awakening, your mission is to awaken others to themselves. Consciousness is undergoing a radical upheaval, and you are part of the vanguard of people who are helping to bring in the new energy. We are seeing the world differently now, as we begin to understand the Mind of God. Aquarius, your higher destiny is to open eyes and hearts to the truth of our humanness. We are spiritual beings having a human experience, and the upheaval is about the realization of this fact. Spirit is acknowledging our connection, the field of consciousness in which we live. Being human is no longer about separateness, but about living as part of the one whole. Helping share this understanding is your higher destiny, your promise, and your potential.

You are: humanitarian, friendly, detached, honest, loyal, original, inventive, gregarious, unorthodox.

You can learn from your opposite sign: Leo can teach you to have greater belief in yourself, realize the gifts you have to offer, and to stand proud and know you are valuable as a member of the collective and as an individual. You can take a leaf from Leo's book, and expect to be validated. Stop apologizing for who you are and feeling the odd one out because you don't fit the common mold. Celebrate your ability to see beyond the safety zone of the status quo.

Some of your symbols in the outer world are: the planet Uranus, waves, technology, electricity, long-distance flying birds, aluminum, kiwi fruit, limes, fruit trees, the shins, the calves, the ankles, the circulatory system, astrology, and the colors electric blue and turquoise. Russia, Sweden, Iran, and New Zealand are Aquarius countries; Moscow and Hamburg are Aquarius cities.

Your body and spirit need you to: reach out and connect, share the power, communicate, walk and run in the wind, liberate yourself from the confines of nine-to-five, find your uniqueness in your work, awaken others to the truth, help heal through the power of your words and your intuition, still your mind through meditation, sleep more, think less.

Your soul needs you to: realize the gifts you have are to be shared for the good of the collective. Yours is a humanitarian mission, and you need to overcome resistance to helping others. Don't stand back feeling misunderstood. You may be, but that is only because you are ahead of your time—and it matters not. Your responsibility is to enlighten and awaken others to the new energy—not to hold back for fear of being thought strange. Yours is a mission of the soul and always has been, and you may neglect it purely out of fear. Fear tries to keep you on the straight and narrow path, the conventional path—but this is not where you need to be. Embrace your uniqueness: celebrate it and share it with whomever you can. There are enough cogs in the machine—you are not to be another of them. Resist the fear that would have you play a role here that is less than you are. Relax your fears around security and survival. You have not been given that direct link to the higher mind for nothing. Use it, speak out, reach out, be the one your heart knows you are. Your mind is brilliant and words are your tools. Convey the messages the world is now ready to hear. This is your promise and your potential.

Pisces

Your higher destiny is to detach yourself from the past and surrender yourself for love. A love not derived from desire, neediness, or insecurity—but love of a higher kind. Love without bounds, transcendental love.

Your journey is essentially a journey to your own heart. There you will discover the flaws of human love; and through a process of annihilation of your own weaknesses, you are destined to create—in this lifetime if you choose—a love that is pure and unconditional. This is the love the masters Buddha and Jesus demonstrated. It is a love that sees beyond differences, and beyond disappointments, hurts, and ego slights; it is a love that says "whatever you do is okay." There are no boundaries with this love, and your mission is to embody this love. This is a path for a master—and may be too much for many. But it is the higher destiny of the evolved Pisces.

You will need to relinquish attachment to the past—that is, memories and patterns, past hurts, old grievances and regrets. These are not required on the path of unbounded love. These all-too-human weaknesses become obstacles and sources in themselves of unnecessary pain and suffering.

Your esoteric ruler is Pluto: Pluto, the god of destruction and the great transformer. Pluto's power is available to you, and the message is: you need to destroy those aspects of your nature that would keep you bound to the earthly chain of suffering. Let go of the small and selfish desires of the ego to be loved, supported, looked after, respected—and know that spirit alone is capable of supporting you and love is already in you, because this is your true nature. Love yourself first. You need no other to feel love; it is all around you. When you discover this truth, you release expectation and surrender to wherever life takes you, surrendering to whomever love sends for you—loving them wholeheartedly and unconditionally. This is your promise and your potential.

You are: sensitive, imaginative, compassionate, kind, intuitive, creative, escapist, dreamy.

You can learn from your opposite sign: Virgo can teach you to apply yourself to work on the details rather than continually escaping into the boundless beyond. You are living here on the planet, and it is here you must act. Virgo knows the importance of the analytical mind. You find it too easy to be swept away by the abstract; look to Virgo's groundedness, and amalgamate your boundless vision with a practical, more organized approach. You would do well to try to integrate Virgo's work ethic and discipline into your own nature. The midpoint of Virgo and Pisces can be a place of deep truth—amalgamating self-discipline and refinement to an awareness of the boundless, the birthplace of creativity.

Some of your symbols in the outer world are: the planet Neptune, poetry, dance, films, make-up, alcohol, fish, water mammals, aquamarines, moonstones, bloodstones, water lilies, willows, figs, cucumbers, the feet, and the colors sea-green, pale blue, mauve, and violet. Portugal, Scandinavia, and the Mediterranean are Piscean places; Jerusalem, Alexandria, and Seville are Piscean cities.

Your body and spirit need you to: swim, bathe, soak—water is your element, so be in it or near it and watch the changing moods of the ocean. Walk by a river or lake or in the rain. Do yoga—feel the union of body and spirit. Meditate regularly; dance; retreat; create an altar in your home, a place of peace away from the world; light a candle, make love by candlelight; keep conscious; love wholeheartedly.

Your soul needs you to: surrender your expectations and old patterns, and be open to loving in a new way. Old programming based on fears of being alone, of not surviving, are no longer relevant. The world is changing, and those old survival patterns are keeping you from expressing the higher connections you have the potential of creating. Yours is a journey of surrender of the ego through consciousness of it. The ego keeps us feeling separate and fearful. When you have destroyed the fears the ego generates, you will be open to love in a much bigger, freer way. This may mean galvanizing your passive response and taking a stand, getting out of situations that are damaging to your sensitive soul, putting boundaries in place and trusting that something better is waiting for you. Restrictions and pain around love are always about the ego; the ego closes down the heart, and your mission is to open the heart. Surrender sounds like sacrifice—it is related, but is a higher octave. Sacrifice implies losing something. In surrender you release only what doesn't serve you; you do not lose anything you really need. Surrender is more of a "letting go" than anything else. The irony is that, in surrender, in letting go of expectations and consciously releasing patterns that do not serve you, you draw to you all the good the universe has for you. You often prevent what you most need coming to you, because you are not willing to put down what you are holding. Your challenge is to release, let go, surrender, and love wholeheartedly. This means to trust in the plan for life, to move yourself into a clearer space, to release the expectations that have held you captive. Becoming more conscious, more loving—this is the mission of all the signs, but for you, Pisces, it is your ultimate higher destiny, your promise and your potential.

Liberating the Self

*The true value of a human being is determined primarily
by the measure and the sense in which he has attained
liberation from the self.*
—Albert Einstein

The esoteric wisdom has said we make our way around the wheel of the zodiac, lifetime by lifetime. Each time we reincarnate, we embody the next Sun sign from the one we have most recently experienced. In this way, the lessons come to us in a succession that follows the logic of the evolutionary intent.

We begin with the Aries impulse to protect our bodies and to use them in exploring the world. The intent of the self is uppermost, and this is the primary motive of the Sun-sign Aries. Our spiritual development continues on, corresponding to the physical and emotional development of each lifespan: from the young child (Taurus through Cancer) to the teenager (Leo) to the young adult and adult (Virgo through Scorpio), through to midlife (Sagittarius) and the autumnal years (Capricorn and Aquarius)—finally surrendering the body in the Piscean phase.

On a soul level we integrate the learning of one sign and then more, on to the next through successive lives. The Sun sign we are living with this time around is, then, the perfect one for us. We are being invited, by the Infinite, to learn the lessons intrinsic to that sign.

We need to ask ourselves: are we learning those lessons? Are we becoming liberated from our smaller selves and moving to a higher place? Are we expressing a positive manifestation of our sign's principles, and are we living a life of integrity or wholeness?

We have been given all we need in this life to do exactly that. If we are awake, that is. For example, if we are playing with a Gemini Sun in this life, we are naturally moved to "be Gemini" (the signs can be used as adjectives just as well as nouns). We embody Gemini in our constant movement, seeking new knowledge and making connections. Life is endlessly fascinating to Gemini Suns.

But the sense of wonder, which is Gemini's life blood, needs to be nourished. If it isn't, Gemini can turn cynical. A "stuck in a rut" Gemini is not honoring the spirit of the sign. We may know Gemini people who have been burned by life, had their trust damaged. They choose to stay stuck in old patterns rather than take the risk to be curious again. They have become embittered; they are no longer fascinated by life, they no longer wonder.

Being true to ourselves means honoring our Sun signs and living authentically, fully engaging in life. We must do so throughout our lifespan. Wonder is not just for children. Neither is fearlessness (Aries), joy (Leo), creativity (Taurus), or compassion (Pisces).

We have been given the gift of this life, and we are charged to use it well. Using it well means being true to the spirit we came in with. It is not the whole truth to say spirit is our Sun sign—but our Sun sign is the centralizing, mobilizing energy and the guiding light for our spirit to find expression in the world. We are more truly ourselves when we choose to be the living embodiment of our Sun sign.

Looking at the signs on either side of our own can be enlightening. Often we are attracted to people in signs on either side of our own. We can see what we have most recently been "working on," where we are now, and the learning we have in store next time; there is an affinity between people whose signs are juxtaposed. As I've been saying throughout, each sign compensates for and includes the one that went before. Individuals in Pisces, the last sign, are not necessarily any more evolved or advanced than those in the Aries phase, because the wheel has no beginning or end—as long as we are on it. But what it does mean is that Piscean people are more consciously aware of the unity and connectedness of life, of the thread that binds all, while Aries people are more consciously aware of the need to look after their own interests and to physically survive. Each sign has a different set of learning requirements, a different energy to resonate with. And that is as intended. The signs were a good idea, in the Mind of God. Progressing, lifetime to lifetime, through each of them exposes the soul to every principle the physical world has to offer. All are part of the grand plan as we make our way back to the Infinite.

Once we have reached a stage in our evolution where we have reached individuation, we have attained liberation from the Self. Our astrology, then, naturally finds a higher expression. We reside on the higher ground. We accept whatever astrology we are born with and the vicissitudes of life that accompany it. Astrological law no longer hurts us. We are, in a sense, beyond it. Most of us, however, are not quite there yet.

There is a saying, "Be kind, everyone is walking a hard road." Astrology helps us see the truth of that. We are all walking a hard road. We all have our gifts and our crosses to bear. We are all diamonds in the rough, and our lives are largely about polishing off the dross to reveal the beauty within: liberating the beauty of the Infinite within the self.

As we journey from lifetime to lifetime, through the signs of the zodiac, we are given the blessings and responsibilities of the vibratory frequency of our Sun signs. Our souls assimilate the lessons we encounter and then we move on to the next class. Life, on a soul level, is very long. This one lifetime is a brief flicker in the eye of eternity. But it is, for all that, infinitely precious. Every moment is a moment to treasure, a moment not to be wasted.

Wasted is all the time not spent in loving . . .

We are going to make mistakes, many of them. We are going to walk around unconsciously a lot of the time. The essential thing is to capture consciousness when it comes, be still, release thought (predominantly fear and all the negative emotions that arise therefrom), and simply rest in the presence of the moment, in the spaciousness of the Infinite. This detachment from the madness of the world of form, the return to the formless, the surrender to the Nowness of the moment, is an act of trust in the intelligence of life.

It is also a return to the "mother" or "goddess consciousness": the yin energy that was overpowered by the yang of the patriarchy and the rise of ego (both being about external power). Yin is not about power. It is about the nurturing, centering energy of the feminine principle—and we urgently need to re-awaken the yin energy on the planet at this time. The yin energy of the goddess consciousness, the mother, is where true power lies. The "power" of the ego-driven values we have been worshipping (in the current system) is hollow and illusory. This, we are on the verge of discovering.

We are heading into a new consciousness. The intelligence that created the whirl of the constellations, the spin of the planets, and the rhythm of a heartbeat is the one intelligence that has a plan and a pattern for our lives. It is not deceived by the illusions of power and ego. We are all cells in the vast body of the Infinite, and that body has a feminine spirit.

Everything happens for a reason. We do not always know what we need or what we are here to learn—and whatever it is, it is part of the mystery. All we need to know is we live in a compassionate universe and there is a plan. If we have a relationship with the Infinite, we do not need to look for our purpose. We need only look within and relax into life, aligning our will with the will of the divine. And from that place, it will find us.

The Infinite, the One, comes through in the love we feel in our hearts—and we can never be lost from such love. The Infinite is both the father and the mother, and it loves us because we are part of it; we are its creations. Our journey from lifetime to lifetime is about the refining of the individual spark of the divine we each carry. The best we can do is turn inward, find the spark that ignites our spirit, and uncover our soul intentions for this life. We have a particular destiny, a unique part to play in the holographic universe. This is all we need to awaken to.

"To be awake is to walk the border between control and abandon," said Carlos Castaneda.

Now is the time to wake up and to walk that border between control and abandon, responsibility and transcendence—not only for ourselves, but for the sake of those who come along after us, as well as for our planet. We are living in a critical passage of evolution, a crucial time for our earth and for ourselves. It is time to wake up, if we are not awake already, and realize the power available to us through our own consciousness. It is time to stop living on automatic pilot, time to stop leaving decision making to those in charge (abandon). We are all in charge. We are all creators, and therefore we are all responsible (control) for the state of the planet and everything living within its biosphere. The choices we make, individually and collectively (they are one and the same in the end), now, this year, are creating our future way of life. The choices we make within our relationships will have an impact on our children that reverberates down through the years within the hearts and minds of those impressionable and defenseless ones. It is time to grow up and act with greater consciousness, in all our relationships. We are affecting far more lives than we can imagine. And every choice we make to use our energy wisely, and the energy of the earth wisely, will take us either to a future heaven on earth, the new earth, or a future disaster (dis-aster = against the stars!).

It is time to go with our stars, align ourselves with our souls, and move to the higher ground. It's time to become more conscious. The time is now. And it may be later than we think!

Thank you for reading the words in this book. May they be for you the gift to your soul they were intended to be.

Afterword

The aim of life is to live,
and to live means to be aware,
joyously, drunkenly, serenely, divinely aware.
—Henry Miller

I would like now to offer you a hint of future attractions. The Sun signs reveal an important aspect of our character, but they are only one aspect of it. To see the full picture, you might like to have your birth chart interpreted by a professional astrologer.

The birth chart is your blueprint, if you like, for this life. It is a symbolic representation of the journey you are on this time around. The Sun, as we have seen, depicts the conscious energy, or fuel, that you need to get you going. It shows where your energy is most appropriately expressed. The Moon (its sign and house position) tells the story of your deepest needs and your emotional disposition. Mercury describes your mental processes, how you think and communicate. Venus is largely your relationship story, and speaks of what you need to feel secure. Mars is the "go" planet: it describes where you direct your drive to survive, what arouses your fighting spirit. Jupiter is where you seek reward, and where life will offer you opportunity for growth and expansion. Saturn is the karmic story—what you fear, where you need to apply yourself and discipline yourself in order to achieve and overcome anxiety and inadequacy.

The outer planets—Uranus, Neptune, and Pluto—describe the collective energies of your generation, and where they are located in your natal chart point to the areas of life where the collective will touch you most deeply. These are the forces of the shadow, the intuition, and of spiritual awareness. And there are other sensitive points in the chart that describe in great detail the karmic patterns you have come in to resolve—your past life story, the chart behind the chart, so to speak.

The relationships each of the planetary bodies have with each other are like aspects of your psyche in dialogue. If they flow well together, the needs those planets represent are met in healthy, productive ways. If they are in an antagonistic relationship, then more effort (consciousness) will be required to integrate those needs. Sometimes this can be a lifetime's work.

Knowing the lifetime's work is half the battle won. An astrologer who can help you clarify the themes you are working on, the karmic patterns you have come in with, is acting as an emissary from the Mind of God. He or she is a messenger from beyond this realm. Astrology is a sacred science. It can be a knowledge system with definite signs that have distinct meanings (in a mind sense), and it can also be an intuitive art, symbolically weaving a story that has deep personal significance and meaning (in a heart sense). Astrology operates on many levels. It transcends the rational mind, even as it includes it. It is one tool, of many, that has the power to guide you to the center of your being and to the purpose of your existence.

A most exciting area, and one that has been largely untapped, is relationship astrology. To put the birth charts of two people who are involved as a couple together reveals information that is truly breathtaking.

Relationships, as we all know, are often difficult. One of the reasons is that so much of what we bring to them is outside of our consciousness. We bring a litany of "old stuff" in the form of historical patterns from childhood, expectations and programs on "how relationships should be" from our past and from the culture we are living in. We burden our relationships with our lack of understanding about ourselves. Relieving this burden is astrology's gift. It helps us to see the patterns within us, which we inevitably project onto our partners.

And relationship astrology can help us see the energies we are working with together in our relationship. All intimate relationships have a karmic legacy; we have been together in former lifetimes, and if we are sufficiently conscious, we can discover what the essence of our relationship was, and is, and what we didn't understand then. We can make intentions and take action to learn the "skipped lessons" (which is what relationship karma amounts to) this time around.

Soul works through relationship. Nowhere in life is the soul experienced quite so profoundly. Understanding your relationships through astrology is a way to reach deeply and insightfully into the territory of the soul.

In our relationships, as in life, there will always be times when we feel completely alone. But remember: the soul's clue is there in the word: *alone* = all one. We are, in fact, all one, even when we feel most alone. Underneath the surface of separateness, there is a thread that connects us. It is more than a thread; it is a blanket, a cosmic blanket—which gives us our life and sustains us through every moment we are breathing on the planet. It is the blanket our consciousness will sink into when we relinquish our bodies and move on into the next dimension. Consciousness, as Deepak Chopra says, is the most permanent thing about us, the one aspect we can expect to continue.

Meanwhile, as long as we are here, we can encourage consciousness to grow by opening our minds and hearts to the soul. We can choose to listen to the soul speak, to have a relationship with the Infinite, to live a symbolic life, and so to deepen our experience of ourselves as we move through our life's journey.

May your life's journey be made richer and more meaningful, and your relationships more joyous and loving, through your decision to open your consciousness to the Infinite within you.

Remember that we are all in this together: what affects one, affects all. It is not only for ourselves we become more conscious, it is for everyone—and for our beautiful planet. Blessings to us all.

Love and Light,
Linda

Notes

Chapter One

1. Deepak Chopra, *Life After Death* (London: Rider & Co., 2006), 53.

2. James Hollis, *Finding Meaning in the Second Half of Life* (New York: Gotham Books, 2005), 179.

Chapter Two

1. Astrophysicist and esoteric researcher Giuliana Conforto wrote in her book *Organic Universe* (Rome, Italy: Edizioni Noesis, 2004):

   We have to remember that the luminous matter we observe with our instruments is only 0.5 percent of all calculated mass. What we see with our eyes is still less. "Reality" is a thin "film" of electromagnetic light, a visible matrix, our biological body or robot can interact with . . .

2. Marsilio Ficino, "De Vita Coelitus Comparanda—How Life Should Be Arranged According to the Heavens," *The Planets*, chapter 23. Quoted in Thomas Moore, *The Planets Within:*

Marsilio Ficino's Astrological Psychology (Lewisburg, PA: Bucknell University Press, 1982), 27.

3. Gregory Szanto, *The Marriage of Heaven and Earth: The Philosophy of Astrology* (London: Arkana, 1985), 105.

Chapter Three

1. James Hollis, *Finding Meaning in the Second Half of Life* (New York: Gotham Books, 2005), 41.

Free Catalog

Get the latest information on our body, mind, and spirit products! To receive a **free** copy of Llewellyn's consumer catalog, *New Worlds of Mind & Spirit,* simply call 1-877-NEW-WRLD or visit our website at www.llewellyn.com and click on *New Worlds.*

LLEWELLYN ORDERING INFORMATION

Order Online:
Visit our website at www.llewellyn.com, select your books, and order them on our secure server.

Order by Phone:
- Call toll-free within the U.S. at 1-877-NEW-WRLD (1-877-639-9753). Call toll-free within Canada at 1-866-NEW-WRLD (1-866-639-9753)
- We accept VISA, MasterCard, and American Express

Order by Mail:
Send the full price of your order (MN residents add 6.5% sales tax) in U.S. funds, plus postage & handling to:

Llewellyn Worldwide
2143 Wooddale Drive, Dept. 978-0-7387-1558-2
Woodbury, MN 55125-2989

Postage & Handling:

Standard (U.S., Mexico, & Canada). If your order is:
$24.99 and under, add $3.00
$25.00 and over, FREE STANDARD SHIPPING

AK, HI, PR: $15.00 for one book plus $1.00 for each additional book.

International Orders (airmail only):
$16.00 for one book plus $3.00 for each additional book

Orders are processed within 2 business days.
Please allow for normal shipping time. Postage and handling rates subject to change.

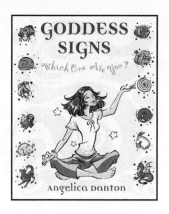

Goddess Signs
Which One Are You?

ANGELICA DANTON

Discover your inner goddess!

Angelica Danton is a friendly guide on the road to self-discovery, helping women tap into their own goddess power. A professional astrologer for twenty years, she has discovered a fascinating correlation between the Chinese zodiac and characteristics of ancient goddesses. The result is twelve Goddess Signs that help women understand their goddess potential.

Learning the characteristics of each Goddess Sign facilitates insight into relationships, work, health, childhood, and spirituality. Recommended magical symbols, lucky numbers, colors, ritual robes, tarot cards, incense, and herbs are also included for each sign.

978-0-7387-0469-2 • 288 pp. • 7½ x 9⅛ • $14.95

To order, call 1-877-NEW-WRLD
Prices subject to change without notice
Order at Llewellyn.com 24 hours a day, 7 days a week!

Astrology for Beginners
A Simple Way to Read Your Chart

JOANN HAMPAR

Getting a glimpse of your own astrological chart isn't a challenge these days. The tough part is finding meaning in this complex diagram of symbols.

In *Astrology for Beginners*, Joann Hampar shows that interpreting your birth chart is actually easy. Emphasizing a practical approach, this step-by-step guide takes you effortlessly through the language of astrological symbols. As each chapter unfolds, a new realm of your horoscope will be revealed, including chart patterns, zodiac signs, houses, planets, and aspects. By the last lesson, you'll be able to read and interpret your chart—what originally looked like a jumble of symbols—and gain valuable insight into yourself and others.

978-0-7387-1106-5 • 240 pp. • 6 x 9 • $14.95

Astrology & Relationships

Techniques for Harmonious Personal Connections

DAVID POND

Take your relationships to a deeper level. There is a hunger for intimacy in the modern world. *Astrology & Relationships* is a guidebook on how to use astrology to improve all your relationships. This is not fortunetelling astrology, predicting which signs you will be most compatible with; instead, this book uses astrology as a model to help you experience greater fulfillment and joy in relating to other people. You can also look up your planets, and those of others, to discover specific relationship needs and talents.

What makes this book unique is that it goes beyond descriptive astrology to suggest methods and techniques for actualizing the stages of a relationship that each planet represents. Many of the exercises are designed to awaken individual skills and heighten self-understanding, leading you to first identify a particular quality within yourself, and then to relate to it in others.

978-0-7387-0046-5 • 416 pp. • 7½ x 9⅛ • $21.95

Cosmic Karma

Understanding Your Contract with the Universe

Marguerite Manning

Marguerite Manning invites you on a spirited ride through the stars to see your soul's evolutionary journey. Based on astrology, *Cosmic Karma* can help you navigate the karmic crossroads and gain fresh insights into your soul's spiritual agenda.

Where has your soul been and what are your karmic obligations in this lifetime? All the answers are in a celestial map of planetary energies—your birth chart. The Sun's house will help you figure out your "cosmic calling"—what you're meant to accomplish, while Saturn, the humorless taskmaster, reveals karmic lessons you need to learn. Finally, peek inside the forbidding and intoxicating twelfth house—where you can explore precious experiences, painful memories, and all your past deeds.

978-0-7387-1054-9 • 216 pp. • 7 x 7 • $15.95

To order, call 1-877-NEW-WRLD
Prices subject to change without notice
Order at Llewellyn.com 24 hours a day, 7 days a week!

Cosmic Trends
Astrology Connects the Dots

Philip Brown

What does astrology have to do with Apple computers, Harry Potter, Bob Dylan, and *American Idol*? According to Philip Brown, trends in technology, film, books, TV, music, and fashion are all influenced by planetary movement. *Cosmic Trends* discusses the startling impact Pluto, Neptune, and Uranus have had—and continue to have—on our evolving culture.

Tracing the outer planets as they travel through the zodiac signs, Brown uncovers amazing cosmic patterns and their link to the sexual revolution, the rise in health awareness, Internet addiction, wireless technology, advertising saturation, and other cultural trends. He offers exercises that help readers develop "intuitive awareness" in drawing their own connections between the planets and world events. Profiles of William Shakespeare, Clara Barton, Martha Graham, Nelson Mandela, and others illustrate how planetary forces have touched their lives and their generations. Fascinating forecasts and a glimpse of what to expect in 2020 are also included.

978-0-7387-0992-5 • 240 pp. • 6 x 9 • $14.95

Soul Mates & Hot Dates
How to Tell Who's Who

Maria Shaw

Do you share a past-life connection with someone special? Are you hoping to reconnect with your soul mate? In this down-to-earth, enlightening guide to karmic partnerships, Maria Shaw characterizes the many types of soul-mate connections and offers advice on how to recognize your special someone.

Reuniting for love, paying a karmic debt, righting a wrong, or completing a higher purpose . . . there are many reasons why souls choose to meet again. True experiences of the author and her clients illustrate the dynamics of these powerful relationships that often involve our lovers, friends, and family. Maria Shaw also shares advice for achieving spiritual love, finding your soul's purpose, ending an abusive relationship, and seeking out the soul mate of your dreams.

978-0-7387-0746-4 • 216 pp. • 6 x 9 • $12.95

Star Guide to Weddings
Your Horoscope for Living Happily Ever After

April Elliott Kent

Do you want a "rockstar" Leo marriage or an enduring Taurus union? Wedding planning mixes with astrology in *Star Guide to Weddings*—a cosmic cocktail of marriage insight based on the Sun sign of your wedding day.

You can't choose your Sun sign, but you *can* choose the sign of your marriage! This adorable, fun-to-read guide takes you through every sign of the zodiac, describing how each can flavor your new life as a married couple. See how your career, health, children, creative spirit, friends, spiritual beliefs, and the overall "personality" of your marriage can be influenced by the stars.

978-0-7387-1169-0 • 264 pp. • 5 x 6 • $12.95

Star Guide to Guys
How to Live Happily With Him . . . or Without Him

ELIZABETH PERKINS

Is your hot yoga instructor a high-strung Virgo or a sensitive Pisces? Could the cutie in the coffee shop be the Leo of your dreams? Thanks to astrology, women can get the nitty-gritty on a crush before leaping into the murky depths of a relationship.

Star Guide to Guys dishes out the lowdown on men in all twelve Sun signs—covering their strengths, challenges, goals, desires, and other personality traits. Women can also depend on this entertaining, easy-to-use guide for insight into their own sign: what they're looking for in a mate, relationship needs, and dynamic compatibility with each sign. For ladies on a break from the dating scene, there's also astrological advice for living a fabulous single life and loving it.

978-0-7387-0954-3 • 240 pp. • 6 x 9 • $12.95

Also available in Spanish

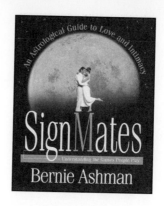

SignMates

Understanding the Games People Play

Bernie Ashman

It is mystery and intrigue that leads many of us to play the relationship game, regardless of how our Sun signs are supposed to get along. *SignMates* dispels the myth that only certain Sun signs are compatible with each other. Any two signs can learn to establish a reliable stability. This book will show you how.

The "game" is defined as a repetitive pattern of negative behavior that interferes with the harmony of a partnership. It is an imbalance of energies, often of a subconscious nature. Take, for example, the "Missing the Boat" game played by Aries and Gemini. It begins when these two fast-paced signs continuously frustrate one another's actions and ideas. Aries' desire to follow immediate impulses clashes with the Gemini instinct to think before leaping. The challenge is to acknowledge one another's needs and potentials. By working through the strategies suggested for your sign combination, you can turn your differences into assets rather than liabilities. This book will help you to better navigate your romantic encounters and create more effective ways to communicate.

978-1-56718-046-6 • 504 pp. • 7½ x 9⅛ • $21.95

Astrology
Understanding the Birth Chart
A Comprehensive Guide to Classical Interpretation

KEVIN BURK

This beginning- to intermediate-level astrology book is based on a course taught to prepare students for the NCGR Level I Astrological Certification exam. It is a unique book for several reasons. First, rather than being an astrological phrase book or "cookbook," it helps students to understand the language of astrology. From the beginning, students are encouraged to focus on the concepts, not the keywords. Second, as soon as you are familiar with the fundamental elements of astrology, the focus shifts to learning how to work with these basics to form a coherent, synthesized interpretation of a birth chart.

In addition, it explains how to work with traditional astrological techniques, most notably the essential dignities. All interpretive factors are brought together in the context of a full interpretation of the charts of Sylvester Stallone, Meryl Streep, Eva Peron, and Woody Allen. This book fits the niche between cookbook astrology books and more technical manuals.

978-1-56718-088-6 • 368 pp. • 7½ x 9⅛ • $19.95

To order, call 1-877-NEW-WRLD
Prices subject to change without notice
Order at Llewellyn.com 24 hours a day, 7 days a week!